# COLLECTANEA

The Second Collection of Poetry
and Narratives

Chapters Writers

2023

## Disclaimer

Some of the stories are personal experiences, but in the works of fiction, any resemblance to actual events or persons, living or dead, is entirely coincidental.

Cover by Helen Iles, Linellen Press

Linellen Press
265 Boomerang Road
Oldbury, Western Australia
www.linellenpress.com.au

We, the authors of this anthology, acknowledge the Wadjak Noongar people and Elders on whose land the members of Chapters meet, sit, speak and write. It was Noongar country in the past, is now and always will be.

**Editors**:

Pamela (PJ) Mistilis, Elizabeth Pappas, Mimma Tornatora, and Hilary Williams

Inquiries should be addressed to the editors.

Chapters is proudly supported by

5 Mackie Street, Victoria Park
Western Australia 6100

# Preface

Dear Reader,

Chapters' second Anthology stands as a testament to the success of this unique group of writers who gather weekly at the Hub in Victoria Park. Founded by me in 2017 and with the support of Lacey Healey, Lynette-Kay Lewis and the staff at Connect Victoria Park, Chapters has grown exponentially. Indeed, the assertion that writers, solitary creatures by reputation, need monastic lives of isolation and total silence to write, may be theoretically true. However, the irony is, there comes a time when even the most dedicated recluse is inclined toward the company of their peers. In this way, Chapters provides an invaluable conduit away from aloneness, temptingly inviting writers to share in circumnavigating the minds of other creatives with the purpose of inspiring, providing feedback and fostering encouragement within the group. These I believe, are vital ingredients for aspiring published and unpublished literary enthusiasts.

With a community-focused '*heartbeat*,' Chapters is a place of warmth in changing times while effecting excellence. Therefore, it is through the themes of Australiana, Humour, Reflections, Romance, Travel, Drama, Nature and the Environment, and Ponderings, that we hope you will find within these pages, a rich temple of works, beginning with two special poems by Hilary Williams and Lacey Healey. They wrote these in celebration of our six years together as a writing group.

Please enjoy this literary '*sea of plenty*' from our inspiring writers.

*Elizabeth Pappas*
*Chapters Founder*

# Poem for Year Six

In the back room of the Hub, we hold our growing club.
Tales and rhymes abound and friendships we have found.

Now at the age of six, we still want our Friday fix,
and as we sit here on our bums, in the room it fairly hums.

We get up and we spout, that is what it's all about.
To write it seems we're driven. 'Tis Nirvana and our heaven.

Our works to stand and deliver, give up, something we could never.
For us no second-rate stuff, original works we have enough.

Sad, happy, thoughtful, deep and some that send us off to sleep.
We get up and have our say, but more than ten, there's hell to pay.

Remember those who've stayed and gone with long and deep affection,
Their contributions short and long worthy of deep reflection.

Stalwart Lacey left this year, but really did not disappear.
When she settles there'll be work, for in her brain I'm sure they lurk.

The list is getting longish with those who've come and gone-ish,
but our club goes on in time and is truly yours and mine.

Hilary Williams – June 2023

# Response

Super-duper words indeed, and humble thanks for noting me.
To think that six whole years have passed is craziness on levels vast.

>There are some people there I know,
>and some of whom I do not know,
>So, life goes on with every blink,
>and writers write, and writers think.

Chapters, though, is quite unique in how it happens every week.
A girl named Libby made it so, a vision she had long ago.

>Indeed, there's sometimes hell to pay,
>but more like herding cats I'd say,
>But all with laughter joy and fun,
>escaping from the week's humdrum.

I loved my time at Chapters real, it had its fun, it had appeal,
From 30 June, six years ago, to leaving Perth for Eastward ho.

But I am still not far away, as virtual life comes into play.
You really can't get rid of me with all of this technology.

>A great big happy sixth from me
>and happy anniversary
>To all who've gathered there this day,
>I raise my glass from far away.

Lacey Healey – June 2023

# Contents

## Australiana



## Humour

# Reflections



# Romance

# AUSTRALIANA

# The Message Tree

I saw you standing all alone
In a barren landscape where nothing was growing
A grey skeleton no longer bearing leaves –
A gaunt figure in a vast landscape.

In your isolation how lonely you look
Your slender grey branches and gnarled fingertips
Point into the distance
As time passes you by.

I know there was at least one time
When company came to you
With brush and paint tin in their hand
Your trunk was painted blue.

Unable to express in words
Your message indelibly clear
You wanted to bring to our attention
Seek help for your pain and fear.

And so your life has taken a different course
A beacon to remind us all
That there is compassion in this world;
Reach out … for a helping hand awaits.

Dorothy Littmann

# Shear Truth

In the early 1960s, three shearers were returning to the big smoke, having completed a long run in the Yalgoo area. The contractor delivered them to the train station in the back of a dilapidated, all-purpose, commonly used, poorly sprung small truck known as a 'ring pounder.' This one even had 'luxury' wooden bench seats in the back! Land Rovers were a thing of the future, and the discomfort of this small truck was exacerbated by rough bush tracks. Contractors disallowed shearers' use of their own vehicles for fear of losing disgruntled staff partway through a run. Something to be avoided at all costs.

These trains served the outback and were a lifeline in every way when most roads were still dirt. Plane travel was reserved for Flying Doctor emergencies. These were the days after gold rushes but before iron ore, when Australia purportedly rode on the sheep's back, squattocracy lingered, and both men and women were tough.

The timing of this trip inconveniently corresponded with the return of secondary school children from the stations to the fairly posh boarding schools in the south. The train was packed to over-full, and waiting days for the next was not an option.

The Train Inspector's solution to this shortage of space was to use the very rough, dirty and uncomfortable guard's van for the shearers, himself and an unexpected, very late addition of a cuffed, police-escorted prisoner en route to the Geraldton lock up.

Knowing what was ahead of them, the shearers had stocked

up with a wet hessian sack full of ice and king browns (Eskys were of the future) and a bottle of whisky in case the beer ran out, all to numb some of the discomfort and boredom of the trip.

As the train rattled on, beer was expertly transferred from bottle to body on this warm spring day. The policeman and inspector were offered some, and it would have been un-Australian not to give the prisoner a swig. By the whistle-stop station of Pindan, the occupants were in varying stages of inebriation, and were somewhat unsteady.

The mournful klaxon wailed, the train headed to Mullewa with a sudden lurch and an unsteady inspector heavily hit the rough wooden planked floor on his posterior and let out a god-awful yowl. Expletives engendered no sympathy, and it was not until he painfully dragged himself up the interior wall of the van, that the enormity of the injury became evident. A monumental steel spike nail was noticeably sticking out of his buttocks causing profuse bleeding. A large hardwood floorboard nail had come loose and had been, sadly, strategically placed in location and angle to penetrate the catapulting butt of the hapless inspector.

Copious amounts of blood *did* engender some sympathy and the group decision was to *'do something quickly.'* So o … the shearers' kit was upended, a long-nozzled oil can was emptied and refilled with whisky. Large pliers were produced to extricate the nail, sewing gear normally used to stitch cuts created by the hands of learner shearers on poor undeserving sheep was produced, and of course a couple of pairs of cleanish undies to dress the wound. The Inspector was assisted to resume the floor on his belly, held down by the now uncuffed lusty prisoner, and after a quick anaesthetic nip (by the inspector), competent hands co-operated to remove the foreign body. Whisky then sterilised the deep wound with the nozzle, thrust and pumped into the wound. With a couple of quick fearless stitches, and an applied whisky-soaked undies pad secured with a trouser leg bandage, the task was completed, and the ordeal was mostly over.

At dusk, on arrival at Mullewa, the policeman, who had handled the situation least well, and who had consumed more than his fair share of beer and whisky, was seen at dusk, being supported, and led in cuffs up the dusty road by the prisoner, towards the police holding cells. These were doubtless familiar to him, from times past, used for the stopover in transit to Geraldton prison the next day.


Hilary Williams

# They Don't Listen

Mega campaign trails
advertising boards
false promises made.

Education, nursing and police force
on the backburner
skyrocketing deficit to be diffused,
private schools regaled.

Interviews, debates, Sixty Minutes and the like
tripping around the countryside
*mine is bigger than yours.*

Little said about remote regions,
little said about Nannas and Pops on the bread line,
little said about ecosystems and wetlands
that perish for the sake of modern living.

Little said about petrol hikes,
better to return to the days of yore
you know what I mean!

And so … the cacophony continues,
*Mine is bigger than yours*
my pockets are deeper than yours … so deep …

protected

    in

      an

        offshore

          account.


              Mimma Tornatora

# Oh Shit!



*(Pardon my French!)*

Just this week I rescued some ancient jarrah boards from hungry white ants in order to feed my equally voracious potbellied stove this winter. These boards 30-ish years ago came from the demolished Midland sale yards which I used to attend on an irregular basis. It prompted a memory I believe worth relating.

Several old boys, fit, wizened, rough and tough characters all, regularly attended the yards each sale day – often retirees, Italian, ex shearers or bushies from way back with a few acres, and an old ute with crate and or trailer. The auctioneers treated them empathetically as they sought the skinnier or mildly injured and odd lots, with the intention of on-selling and turning a quid.

One of these guys was perched on a top rail overlooking a pen of temperamental, unhappy, large northern steers undergoing lively bidding from the sundry professional stock buyers. This particular old dude suddenly scuttled down the wooden rails with unbelievable agility into the pen, braved the horned cattle, stooped to the well-trodden, cow-pattied ground, put hand quickly to mouth and, in a twinkle, rescaled the rails before anyone had a clue as to how or why the incident occurred. Gradually the murmuring buyers put some sense into this unusual brief and spectacular event.

'Oh shit!' exploded the auctioneer, midst the gobsmacked crowd. 'His false teeth fell out, and he went and got them!'

My spontaneous comment was: '"Oh, shit!" – exactly the right words!'

Raucous laughter erupted as the implications of the incident sank in. Forever written in my memory, unlike a lot of other things of late.


Hilary Williams

# Ode to an Antique Milk Churn

(*In the manner of Keats*)

Thou much used graceful piece of steel
Ye practical shape of times long past
Two pieces of fitting metal do seal
What gallons of milk held fast.

You've stood so bravely in varied places
Concrete ramp, old trucks and drive
Gravel road and factory spaces
Hard knocks and drops reflect your life.

But now, in pride on my verandah
Like me, with weathered veneer
A woodchip store and pot plant stand
Honoured place, post long career.

Hilary Williams

# Sex in the Sand

Envisage a short stallion pony required to serve a thoroughbred-sized mare, both animals in a large paddock. Solution … use the makeshift, serviceable but seldom-used loading ramp standing about a metre high in the middle of the paddock. With the mare firmly backed up to the base of the ramp and the stallion on the top, his elevation improved the height differential and thus the chances of success. All proceeded according to plan. (God bless riding school nags with a kind temperament, accompanied by an efficient helper.)

However, just at the vinegar stroke, the ramp edge partially crumbled, and down went the stallion, his mighty weapon rampant and well lubricated, into the soft sand below. Thus, when he untangled his legs and stood up, his weapon was coated better than any schnitzel, and then, following nature, he retracted. To this day, I feel for him, and swear he had an

*'I have just sucked a lemon!'* look on his shocked face.

All credit to him, though, as with bush repairs to the ramp, and the forces of nature upon him, a second, successful attempt was made.

This was one of the many fun experiences (but not for the horse!) during the riding school years in Lancelin.

Hilary Williams

# HUMOUR

# The Day I Stood Up for a Pedalfile

One day I was on my way to North Perth Primary School, riding the bike I had recently won at a children's concert in *His Majesty's Theatre* in the city, when suddenly a pedal broke and came off, making it impossible for me to continue riding.

I was right outside the home of Mr Harmes who lived nearby. I had heard people refer to him as a possible pedalfile and I thought that might mean someone who could fix pedals. As he was standing near his front gate, I showed him my broken pedal and he went into his shed and came out with the right tool for the job in his hand – a screwdriver. I tried to keep out of Mr Harmes' way, and he fixed my bike there and then. I thanked him as I rode off and I got to school before the bell rang.

Mum and Dad were very angry and growled at me when I told them what had happened and what I had done. I showed them my bike which looked as good as new. I told them how helpful and friendly Mr Harmes had been and then I promised them I wouldn't do anything like that ever again!

Pauline Weir

# A Riff on a Rhyme

The restaurant is plush: thick carpets, matching chairs, crisp white tablecloths, flowers, mirrors – several notches up from their usual pub. The PA nods approvingly, settles in her seat, allows the waiter to drape her serviette, quite as if she's eaten at places like this all her life. The office baby, fresh from school, has never eaten at a place like this and jumps every time the waiter approaches. The others arrive, Birthday Boy last, and take it all in their stride.

Orders are placed, glasses filled, and the birthday toast made.

'You still want to go to the nightclub?' asks Office Manager.

Birthday Boy nods.

'I like jazz, and this new band is supposed to be very good. I'm going, but you don't have to come.'

'Oh, we're going, we're going! I booked a table at eleven, so tomorrow I plan to be late. Show Sonny Boy we can all roll up when we feel like it.'

Office Baby says: 'But he's the Boss's son. He can get away with things.'

'So can we,' says PA. 'Did you hear the latest – he actually fell asleep *on* his desk. We left him when we went home, and the cleaning crew woke him up!'

They'd all heard; it was just the way this boss's son behaved. They all had examples: he came in late; he left early; his work was late; his reports were incomplete; he missed meetings, and when he was there, he had no idea why, or what for. The tales flew around the table, anecdotes old and new, all far too familiar.

As the wine went down, the noise went up, everyone laughing like drains. The Maître D gestured his staff to hurry the group along.

PA checks her watch. 'What time is the reservation?'

'Eleven.' The Office Manager raises his hand, gesturing for the bill.

The Maître D hurries over, presents it in its little leather folder. He's afraid there will be more commotion as the group sorts out who owes what, but the Office Manager has it under control, and hands over cash, plus a generous tip. There are some hasty but relatively quiet trips to the bathrooms, and the group leaves, arguing about the best way to get to the nightclub, before they pile into taxis.

The crowd outside the nightclub is long. As they wait, they listen to the crowd; many have been before, and everyone is full of praise. Others can only hope to get in. It's obviously popular. PA thanks heaven for the foresight that planned a reservation. If only Sonny Boy could be more like this.

'Think this is how Sonny Boy would have planned things?' she says ironically, and they laugh as they are let inside.

They are led to a corner booth and order more drinks. It's dark, but noisy, but only with chatter. The band is taking a break.

The lights go down; the noise quiets. The band returns; the stage lights up. PA nudges Office Baby.

'Isn't that Sonny Boy? What on earth is he doing here?'

'Shhh!' she shushes.

The band settles, begins playing. Sonny Boy steps forward, raises his Alto Sax; the first glorious notes soar … he's playing the blues.

Irene M Powell

# **Vulnerability and the Snake Oil Detector**

There's a lot of practical help available, if you're really looking. Why, just this week, I have been offered the only way to end back pain forever; the spiritual solution to all my problems; how to lose 10kg a week off my belly; a 20-minute cure for cancer and one hundred ways to raise my beauty goddess. None of these amazing benefits come free, of course, even the new avatar and saviour of the world is seeking a donation for his blessing. At $150 (special offer this week only) it sounds like a great bargain.

And yet …

Once upon a time, back in the days before multiple birthdays, when they were something to actually look forward to, when I was capable of multitasking, i.e., finding my red shoes almost before they were lost, remembering the date *all day long*, booking the cat's inoculations, not losing the car in the carpark; and all at the same time … You remember what that was like, don't you?

Well, as I was saying … what was I saying? Oh yes, back then I had a built-in snake oil detector. This useful little device enabled me to sniff out dodgy real estate persons, second-hand car dealers, smarmy stockbrokers and male dates wearing too much gold jewellery (you know the type). A mere glint in the eye as they viewed my modest three-by-one, my ageing Magna, or a sneak peek at my (admittedly rather trim) ankles, was enough to set off the warning snake oil system in my head. This was in my mother's voice, oddly enough, reminding me that I was on the point of being *taken advantage of,* which quickly put all systems into a fast back pedal. Who knows what catastrophes were avoided by this sneering voice in the back of my head:

*'Yeah, right! In your dreams!'*

Sadly, this kindly protection system no longer works. Maybe I grew out of it, or maybe I just lost it, along with a few other necessary parts of my mind, as the number of candles on my birthday cakes increased to the point of causing entire cake collapse. I am now the original wide-eyed optimist, beloved of estate agents, rising messiahs and insurance agents; and therefore, apparently open to suggestions that age symptoms can be cleared in just ten minutes a day by the purchase of stunningly expensive exercise systems. Or even the latest in body slime tablets, guaranteed to make me sleep like a newborn, drop 5kgs overnight and sing like Lady Gaga. (OK, I put that bit in myself, but you probably get the idea.)

We are all vulnerable as we age. The sharks are cruising out there, hoping for a quick snap at our wallets, and our desire to be fit and strong again is so real that we can easily fall prey. So: develop your snake oil warning system, and don't part with the readies until you are sure that you will be getting exactly what you pay for.

On the other hand, $150 for a blessing from the new messiah … wow! Can I resist that?


Susan Ormrod

# Faith

When we were little, we went to Sunday School every Sunday. We attended the Methodist church, as Dad was a Methodist, and had actually been sworn to temperance at the age of two months. Mum was Anglican, but there was no Sunday School at St Mary's Anglican Church at that time.

I quite enjoyed Sunday School, and I admire Mum and Dad for getting the five of us off to Church every Sunday morning. I guess it could have given them a bit of a break from us, but they were quite staunch in their beliefs. When the new St Mary's Anglican church had been built, we all went to church there, but I remember worrying about Dad feeling left out because he could not take Communion with us and had to remain in the pew. I decided then that I would have any future children of mine baptised into my husband's religion, so he would not feel left out. I did do that, and although he was an altar boy in his youth, my husband is not the slightest bit interested in going to church, although he will go to funerals, weddings and the odd baptism.

Anyway, when I was little, I loved going to church. I loved singing hymns, and listening to Mr Taylor giving the sermon and I would come out of church thinking:

'I want to be good!'

When I was about seven, one of my best friends was the headmaster's daughter, Ruth Torissi. Mr Torissi was a little bit intimidating, although I must say he was always very kind to me. Mrs Torissi was extremely so. One day at school when someone had stolen my lunch, she made me another. I must have been a little slow, or someone else was extremely hungry, because while I was talking to one of my friends, my replacement lunch was stolen!

I would sometimes stay with Ruth and her family over the weekend, and Ruth would sometimes stay with us. This weekend was my turn to stay with her family, and as Ruth and her sister Rita were both in the choir at the Roman Catholic Church, I was sent off to join the congregation. I was given two threepences for the collection but was issued with no information on procedure once I reached the church. As the people filed into the church, I saw them reaching up to a little receptacle. It was placed too high for me to be able to see what was in it, and as everyone reached up to it, I thought to myself:

'This must be where they put their money for the collection,' (I hadn't noticed that they were touching their foreheads with the holy water into which they had just dipped their fingers) so I reached up and dropped my two threepences into the little receptacle. Well, that was one job done. Now to find myself a seat.

I chose an empty pew, closer to the back of the church than the front, but shortly after I had sat down, an elderly lady sat in the same pew.

'My goodness,' I thought, 'this is Aunty Mary Norrish.' Aunty Mary was my Grampa's sister, but we didn't see her often enough for her to recognise me. Grampa used to be Roman Catholic, but converted to Anglican in order to marry my Grandma. He became a staunch pillar of the church, but his siblings remained in the faith.

The service went on, until two men came around the congregation with collection plates. Oh, dear, I had nothing left to give. When one of them reached Auntie Mary, she opened her purse to reveal so many coins, my eyes nearly popped out of my head! If only she knew me and knew of my plight! As he came to me, in a very embarrassed state I said:

'I don't have any.' Not only did I suffer that embarrassment, but he came back a second time, much to my horror. This time he didn't pause in front of me. I was too worried to tell the Torissi family what I had done, but I did tell my parents once I had gone home. My father laughed.

'You shouldn't have let that bother you,' he said. 'In a situation such as that, you just hold one hand over the plate and flick the bottom of the plate with the other. It sounds like coins falling onto the plate, and no one is any the wiser.'

If only I had known *all* the rules *before* I went to that church!!

P. J. Mistilis

# Bend a Little

I'm not broke, just slightly bent – a condition we've all been in at one time or another.

Peter and Paul became quite good friends, if not a little exhausted. Peter paid Paul, and Paul paid Peter – equal opportunity you might say – except when Peter couldn't pay Paul, it became a little messy. Know the feeling?

When Peter couldn't pay Paul, Paul just had to go hungry. When things are tight, we all manage somehow – bread and dripping days maybe?

Let's rejoice in the fact that Peter eventually did pay Paul, and we all lived happily ever after.

Noeline Frost.

# The Frog

I sat on a log, and gazed at a frog
Which seemed to be asking me: 'Why,
When you have roast beef
I sit on a leaf,
And all I can catch is a fly!'

We continued to meet; I looked at his feet –
His toes were so thin and so long!
He leapt from his leaf,
And it beggared belief –
His legs were so muscly and strong!

I missed him one day – he had swum right away:
I wondered: what do I do now?
I waited a while,
And instead of a smile
A frown had indented my brow.

To my delight, he came back one night.
He said: 'Please don't think me a "baddie;"
I've missed you too,
But I've had lots to do,
'Cause I'm daddy to dozens of taddies!'

P. J. Mistilis

# Adam ...

God, said Adam, you want me to what?
Yes, I heard you, but what's the plot?
You can't be serious my dear friend,
For if I do it will be the end.
Adam sat, with his mind in a frenzy
Looking at Eve in all her splendry.
Could he say *yes* to God, but *no* to Eve?
God's way up there so a few days reprieve.
The days passed with his mind in turmoil,
His stomach was now beginning to roil.
I can't do both, but I have to choose
But oh my God so much to lose!
I need an idea, a lightbulb moment
Some idea to end the torment.
Well God's up there and we are here
So let's sit down and have a beer.
I will be a gentleman and let Eve choose
I am a coward and I hate to lose.
Well, said Eve, after much thought
Blow it Adam you are a good sort
So let's tell God that we don't care
He can keep his apple and we'll have a pear!

Elaine Palassis

# Manners and Honesty

Is there or isn't there? – that is the question. This story may not seem quite relevant; however, it comes into my category of honesty or manners.

I don't think it honest or good manners to steal someone else's newspaper. I had always maintained that the first time my Saturday newspaper was stolen, that was it! I would immediately cancel it. Having begrudged the fact that I had felt that I had been pressured into getting it delivered in the first place by an eager vendor going door to door for more business.

So determined was I that my paper would not be stolen, that I would get up before 3.30 Saturday morning to retrieve it before anyone had the chance, so imagine my irritation when I accidentally slept in and didn't wake till 7 am. Luckily for me, I slept with my bedroom windows open, so when I started to glance around for the paper, I was lucky enough to spot it, at the same time as a second person, walking along the footpath. It was half on the footpath and half on the property. The young man who had spotted it thought he had found gold, and was just bending down to reach for it when this booming voice came from out of nowhere:

'Leave that alone! That's mine!'

The young man straightened up; didn't bat an eyelid, and just casually sauntered off in the direction in which he was going without so much as a guilty flush on his face. He knew the paper wasn't his, but wasn't in the least bit bothered.

Some people have no conscience whatsoever.

Apart from being mildly startled, he wasn't at all ruffled,

though I bet he got the fright of his life when he bent down. He wouldn't have expected to have been witnessed!

I laughed to myself, even though I was angry.

I haven't seen the fellow since. He's probably taking another route and someone else's newspaper.

Noeline Frost

# In The Pantry

Food for thought: what is a pantry?
Is it a room, a storage closet, a stockroom, larder or a cubby?
Hundreds of years ago it was called *'panterie'* by the French I read,
Meaning *pain* as it was used to store loads of bread.

Today it's near a kitchen or dining room with a closing door,
And is a cool dark place with plenty of room to store.
All kinds of foods, too many to list all,
Some even hanging on the inside wall.

When feeding your family there's supplies to delight,
Cereals, spices, flour, oils, rice, and even vegemite.
Yet so many tin cans that are out of date on the shelves,
All stacked in, or out, of order, to identify themselves.

There's more than food in most pantries for sure,
Plates, cups, food processing machines are in there to store.
But best of all deep on the shelves are the hidden treats,
Chocolates, wine, and lots of delicious sweets.

So, when my grandchildren visit, I often find,
One or two hiding with the door closed behind.
I wish I could magically restock the messy cubbyhole,
Instead, regular supermarket trips are new in my Gran-role.

Kerry Smith

# Rats

Rats, they fought the dogs and killed the cats!
They bit the babies in their cradles,
Drank the soup from the cook's own ladles –

(Apologies, Robert Browning)!

They also ate our tomatoes, our figs, our guavas and our grapes, our oranges, quinces and our monstera deliciosas. I said to my husband that there was no point in waiting until the fruit was ripe to put out the baits – who would want to eat a bait when the alternative was a sweet and juicy fig? So, this season he put out the baits early, and having done some research, covered them with a slather of peanut paste. It was successful to start with. We saw some slow-moving rodents, which were promptly caught and dispatched to the bin. One was seen floating gracefully in the pool, so he or she was similarly dealt with, and a smell of which we couldn't find the source indicated the demise of a third. Two inconsiderate victims crawled into the cavity of the double brick wall, sadly, next door, in my daughter's house, and demonstrated their discontent by driving the occupants of the house to their parents' home for meals. Luckily, the family could close off the odorous dining and living area of the house when it came time for sleep.

Sadly for us, once the word gets out on the rat vine that there is a vacancy at number thirty-two, other rats are already lined up, rent in hand, for their turn to fill the void. You just can't win!

My friend, when she lived in Mosman Park, laughingly explained to us that although *they* had rats, all her neighbours, not willing to admit that they too had 'rat' problems, declared that *they* had infestations of *possums.*

When we were kids, my two older brothers set off to the grain shed to deal with the rat problem there. Leslie held the spotlight while Brian wielded the air rifle. They were very successful, bagging twenty-one of the finest, which, the next day, were nailed by the tail up on the wall in order of size. Quite impressive.

In our present home, years ago, when we had cats, they kept the rats on their toes. On the hot summer nights, we left windows and doors open to allow a cooling breeze to chase out the heat. At one stage, there was no flywire on the front 'fly screen door'. During the course of one night, we were all woken by a hullabaloo and leapt up to find that our male cat, Nutmeg, had chased a rat through the house, into the bedroom where my sister-in-law slept and had it cornered on the windowsill.

On another occasion, we had friends over and our daughter, Mel, and one of the little boys visiting had gone into the kids' bathroom to fetch some rechargeable batteries which had been charging there, when we heard a bloodcurdling scream. I froze, thinking we had electrocuted our friends' son. 'Face it!' I thought and raced in to see an enormous rat rearing up on the bathmat. It then shot into Mel's bedroom. 'I'll get it,' I thought, visions of mice in my mind, but on looking it in its nasty little eyes, I soon decided perhaps instead, I should get Nutmeg to show it a thing or two. Nutmeg, however, turned up his nose and walked off in disdain, because earlier in the night he had been trying to tell me he'd seen a rat in the house, and I had ignored him. 'If you wouldn't help me then, I shan't help you now!' seemed to be his message.

Fortunately, Arthur, my husband, had by this time fetched the yard broom and came in, pinning it to the wardrobe door, and was able to dispatch it in a bag.

I have dealt with my fair share of mice throughout my younger years, and rabbits were easy enough to help meet their maker, but there is something particularly unsavoury about a rat, and I can't understand people having them for a pet. *I* most certainly never will.

P.S. My husband just said, when I had read this piece to him: 'What about two-legged ones?'

'Good point,' I replied. 'The problem with them is that they are almost impossible to eradicate!'

P. J. Mistilis

# REFLECTIONS

# **Once Upon a Time …**

I noticed her because she was so self-contained. She had no phone, no book, no gossipy friend. She sat quietly, not sad, rather pensive, thoughtful. No waiter service for this independent woman, she had taken her Earl Grey tea and homemade shortbread to a table by the window.

A woman after my own heart. I toasted her with my own tea, a warm delight this morning. She cupped her hands around the cup, sipping gently, just as I did. It was hard not to stare; she could have been me. Once upon a time.

We were almost face-to-face, though I sat at an outside table. The day was chilly with a brisk breeze; spring was coming but it was taking its own sweet time. I huddled gratefully into my warm coat, a lucky find so late into the season. It had done me proud, but I longed to fling it aside for lighter wear. Her coat looked heavy; she wore it open, slipping from her shoulders. Was she doing what my mother insisted I do when I was a girl, opening it up to 'feel the benefit' later? She eased the coat back into place, smoothing down the fur collar. Real? Faux? Whatever, the colour suited her, and she wore it with flair.

I shuffled around. My seat was hard, difficult to move with all my bags clustered around my feet. She had bags too, down by her feet; bags from named stores, no gaudy colours, just discrete names and logos. I wondered what she had bought. I imagined birthday gifts, for family, for friends. A guilty something for herself; but no, that had been me, once upon a time.

We finished our tea at the same time. The day had warmed

up and my time was my own, so I stayed put. Not so for her. She gave one glance at her watch and hurriedly fastened her coat, wrapped a silky scarf around her neck – beautiful silk, heavenly colours – and gathered her bags. No grocery bags, I noticed, perhaps that was for another day. Probably she had a car; could do it all in one trip. Yes, just like me, once upon a time.

She noticed me as she hurried out, gave me a nod and carried her bags to her car. Nice car, I thought, classy. She lifted the bags into the boot, slammed it shut … and came back to me. She unwound her scarf, that beautiful, silky scarf, and gave it to me. It was warm, with a subtle fragrance. I looked at her, bewildered. Most people avoided me, avoided us all, their eyes sliding past, uneasy. I was used to being ignored.

'It's quite warm,' she said. 'Surprisingly so.' She pushed some notes into my hand, 'Get something warm to eat.'

With that, she rushed away, into the car, back to her life.

Ah, yes. That had been me, once upon a time.


Irene Powell

# The Night Flower

My Auntie Cécile,
nicknamed Titile,
by the first little ones
in the family.
A name, resonating
with many fond
and sad memories,
of a time,
when my relatives
lived in the same country,
sharing, caring
supporting one another.

I imagine her,
as a young girl,
slender, pensive, gentle,
the fifth child
in a family
of nine siblings.
The quiet one,
unobtrusive,
unnoticed
until great promise
her delicate fingers
accomplished.

Winning awards
in fine needlework,
lacemaking, crochet
knitting and dressmaking,
propelled her
as the little god-fairy
of the large family.

Her status assured,
her role well-defined
in a patriarchal world.
Her work cherished,
and well-sought-after,
her nimble fingers and mind
never idle
creating marvels
until late hours
by candlelight.

Indispensable,
she became,
earning praise and a living
from her impeccable craft.
So dedicated was she,
unknown to her,
her fate was sealed,
silently, naturally

as a chaperone,
to her younger sister.
Later, a carer
to her ailing mother.
Resigned, compliant,
as she should be,
muted
by decisions from above,
the spinster of the family
bowed her head quietly,
like a night flower.


Marie-Anne Pontré

# Forgetting Over and Over Again

When darkness clouded her thoughts
she forgot how to dance
chose to live alone and ceased to love.

She embraced emptiness
tended the parched rose garden
wrote letters to no one.

She paid utilities that didn't exist
showered in the rain
and applied make up.

She ate chocolate marbled cheesecake
through an intravenous drip whilst
attempting to remove her serial number.

She forgot how to create poetry
with metaphors dancing on the page
she forgot her mother's name.

When darkness clouded her thoughts
she forgot how to dance
forgot how to dream.

Recalling
only the smell of burning flesh
and ash falling from the sky.


Mimma Tornatora

# Rains Too Early

After the first substantial rains … listen to the earth … no; really listen.

Hear the grunt of the swelling seed bursting out, and the crack of the husk giving way?

Roots as legs desperate to stretch down, creaking pale, lengthening with toes burying into soil spaces. Seeking the security of depth.

Simultaneously, multi-shaped, pale green arms reach upward, clapping, applauding the long-awaited freedom at last to use sun, air and moisture to grow.

Sadly, a fortnight later with no more rain, hark the agonised death cries, instant demise as clumsy footed, hungry mouthed, green seeking, scrabbling livestock uproot the desperate growing efforts just made, destroying more than they eat. They too, were keenly awaiting the season break.

But this may be a more merciful death. As rainless days pass, tune to the soft sighing of the remaining parched and thirsty plants as they slip into wilting then rustling demise and finally whispering to the un-shot seeds below:

'Next time, you try.'

It is inevitable in the cycle of rains too early, false hope for plant, animal and farmer.

Hilary Williams

# The Holy Grail

God weaves his tapestry of truth
From before the big bang
Where corruption by vegan wokeness
Each strand a possible admission
Of life that filled dark corners
But God's energy
Remains pristine, pure, beautiful,
To be returned to each new generation
So that they can complete
Covered by God's compassion,
Where each strand the thread
Of God's own tapestry of truth
This is the Holy Grail
Of something beyond
Beyond what we know.

J. K. Baldock

# Fragile Vase

She sits tall, poised
An exquisite crystal vase
Fragile, hesitant

Searching for true love
Shards of sorrow brimming high
On edges of soul

Tender dreams shattered
On wall of narcissism
Scars still palpable

Ten years on, she says
Voice echoing bruised pieces,
Ongoing sorrow.

Marie-Anne Pontré

# Why Home Ran Away from Me

Was it because I didn't clean my teeth?

Was it because I wasn't smart enough?

Was it because I wasn't pretty enough?

No, no, none of these things.

It was because at the age of fourteen my parents decided to move once again for about the twelfth time in so many years.

We lived, at the time, in Waiongana, out in the country, about three miles from Inglewood, a small country town near Mt Egmont in New Zealand, and about a forty-five-minute ride to New Plymouth, a bigger town in Taranaki.

No public transport went past our place, and we didn't own a car.

My father was a carpenter. He rode a bike to the jobs he had in the area. These of course were mostly for farmers, whom he said were often slow to pay. Consequently, we never had much money, though Dad always seemed to have money for the pub, to which he often went.

I digress. The decision to move came at a bad time for me. I was currently in the senior local marching team, and we were about to come into the New Zealand Championships which were to be held in New Plymouth that year. Our instructor, Mr Plumb, had been building up to this for years, and said that this was our year, he was certain of it. We had come second in Christchurch one other time, but it was a matter of pride for Mr Plumb to get a first place.

We were a good team, and I was an integral part in a pivotal spot. My absence would damage the team. It was therefore arranged and agreed between my parents and Mr Plumb that I would stay behind.

I would leave school, which at the time, was no great loss to me. Accommodation was arranged with one of the girls, and a job at McKenzies, a store in New Plymouth where two of the older girls – Cynthia and Valerie – worked. They had talked the manager into taking me on, so at fourteen I embarked on an early entry into the workforce, ill-equipped to handle the world on my own. It was a learning curve to say the least.

I was so good at the job, the manager didn't want me to leave when the time was up.

I was a quick and willing worker, but being away from the family was foreign to me. I didn't cope so well with the strangeness of it all. Prior experiences hadn't made me confident, and even though home wasn't the happiest place to be, it was a known quantity.

Many adventures were had in this period of isolation, not all of them good.

And that, my friends, is how home ran away from me!


Noeline Frost.

# Phoebus

The weak morning sunlight fingers its way
across the lush, uniform green paddock.
Elongated shadows ever shorten
as the orb climbs incrementally.
Almost indiscernible,
but relentless in its rising aspiration.
A practice perfected from the beginning of time.
Warmth not yet manifest, but a unique glow
of winter sun on my east horizon.

Hilary Williams

# A Goodbye

We said goodbye in a bleached hallway
on a plain of red dust
as ruby as us
(did you leave or did I stay?)

Sorrow is piercing white –
not a soft black crevasse
the colour of your eyes and hair
floating in the quilt of night.

We said goodbye in a jagged highway
our lives in the red dust
swirling, a speck. Trust –
love is motion, you say.

My eyelids quiver like the shore
to keep the throbbing waves at bay
A hug, and you ebb away
(are you right, and I wrong?)

There is no help to quell the fears
Time will inch
And Tomorrow I will walk the red earth
Muddy from tears.

Kritika Lama

# A Moonlit Night Down in the Southwest

It was the perfect evening for fishing
in that first week of January 2019.
After a hot summer day,
the cool breeze beckoned families in the bay
on the other side of Bussell Highway.


Boats of all sizes bobbed contentedly on the dark blue ocean
With little children like shadowy figures
frolicking gayly in the receding water,
While parents readied their fishing gear with more beers.


As the declining sun dipped discretely in the west side,
I retraced my steps in the opposite way
furrowing my toes in the furtive ripple.
The dusk-sky on display
was unfurling its open canvas on the water's crest.


On my right lingered
a palette of deep orange and pink brush strokes
while on my left, the pale moon
like a promise, glimmered tentatively above
projecting a beam of silvery light on the darkening ocean.

A couple of fishermen perched gingerly on the rocks,
their rods at the ready for their catch.
I watched bemused as one of them with precision cast his line
Tracing a long arc in the silvery path.

There, under the breath of a moonlit night,
nature's magic was at play
in the vast expanse of the bay.
Within minutes, the fisherman reeled in his line
with great vigour, a quivering fish jittering on its way.

Etched in my mind,
the memory of that night bathed in total tranquillity.
The bay, a symphony of silver shades rippling across the waves.
The moon beaming from above radiantly.

A tide of love, a tide of joy.
A whisper in the infinity of time.
A murmur of gratitude in the recess of my soul.
A prayer.

Marie-Anne Pontré

# Instant Gratification


The sun shines on my naked flesh
as I listen to the chorus
of red-tailed black cockatoos
in the canopy.

~ ~ ~

Children rummage through dress-ups
with smiles on innocent faces.

~ ~ ~

Lovers meander hand in hand
throughout Rome's side streets
leading to the piazza
dazzled with dance and festivities.

~ ~ ~

Metaphors waltz on the page
to the sounds of Funky Town.

~ ~ ~

Nonni reminisce about
simpler days
harvesting grapes and
churning buffalo mozzarella.

~ ~ ~

Hoisted upon angel wings
and carried to a sanctuary of unity.

~ ~ ~

Soft drumming in the yarning circle
accompanied by a smoking ceremony
honouring ancestors
that instilled love for Country.


Mimma Tornatora

# Under the Breath of a Moonlit Night

It was almost midnight and, glancing out through my bedroom window, the moonlight resembled intense sunlight reflecting onto Earth. My surrounds were so radiant I found it hard to believe that this shimmering light was real. How could so much light be mirrored from the dark grey rocky surface of the moon? Thanks to the sun for its reflection onto the moon. Meanwhile, the stars were dulled and distanced. As this full moon felt so close to planet Earth, I could feel it enveloping me.

Being so thankful for my life on Earth, I became so immersed by this mystical light that I escaped outdoors to wander to a nearby botanical garden and submerse myself under the breath of this moon. I remembered a Greek story about Luna, who was the goddess of the full moon in heaven. Maybe she was focused on me, staring upwards to my family ancestors who are now stars in heaven.

I sat on a wooden bench and closed my eyes tight. My heart started beating and I wished I could float up into the sky to be with all, so our souls may meet again and rejoice. My innermost self was calm and quiet as the moon gave me the freedom to meditate and take away any anxiety. Gratitude for the loving life in which my parents engrossed me and allowed me to be the free-spirited individual I am today, as a Mum and a Gran. This full moon with its luminous shining glow empowered and energised me to accept many new challenges in my life.

My thoughts drifted to my early studies about space and the fact that the rocky-bodied moon is Earth's only natural satellite.

Despite being nowhere near as huge as Earth, it has so much control over our planet. It can affect our emotions; it also impacts the ocean tides, light and time. Even birds are known to use the moon for their navigation and migration. Humans have made many small steps with landing on the moon, and now future lunar-based plans by various Space Agencies are being proposed.

With eyes suddenly wide open again, I returned my thoughts to reality and the need to head home and get some rest with the moon viewing me through my bedroom window. Whether it's a full moon, half-moon or another phase, the size of the moon doesn't change, as without the sun, the moon would be completely dark on our Earth.

Being so thankful for my life on Earth and feeling positive and grateful for all that surrounds me, I floated into a deep breathing sleep, with the full moon overhead in the bright night sky.

Kerry Smith

# Upon a Summer Day

Two children's playgrounds sit side by side, separated by a low fence and three magnificent old pines that tower into the sky.

The one on the left puts the other to shame. It belongs to a Holiday Park and is reserved for paying guests. The other is Council owned, with two swings, a modest plastic arrangement of slide, cubby house and climbing frame. There is a drinking fountain, a blue dish supported on a central post from which the water falls, an arrangement which seems to baffle both birds and children and they ignore it.

The other is a children's dream. What to try first? The climbing frame, three sturdy posts, tepee style, with branches crisscrossed to allow a choice of easy or complicated ways to the top.

How about jumping onto the bouncy bladder and just bouncing around? Or climbing the glassed-in steps to whiz down the chute? And use the long chute or the short? Or climb on top of the colourful tube and challenge friends on who can stay on top longer?

And over it all a shade cloth to shelter children from the sun, held aloft by painted poles, yellow, orange and blue. The other playground swelters under the hot sun during the day, the trees only shade the spot when children are at home, bathing away the day before story time and sleep.

On the left, a falling child will land upon a spongy floor, bright and colourful with swirly patterns. On the right, a safety floor, but scuffed a dirty grey-brown from years of use and poor maintenance.

Comfy chairs, thick padded cushions and a snack bar, sheltered by green shade cloth, for the parents on the left, a sturdy but well-worn bench in the harsh sun for the others.

And, unfair as it seems, the paying guest can pass the fence and use the other swings, the climbing frame, and deny the others their turn.

And so, the days pass one by one, the playgrounds are used, and well used. But do the children on the right look left and yearn? Or do they enjoy what they have and get on with enjoying their days?

Irene M Powell

# We are Eternal Beings

Aside from our humanness, we are eternal beings who live in our physical bodies which come with each rebirth with purpose. What that purpose is for us to achieve during that new life upon where we are born and what country, what family traditions etc., is 'a complete mystery,' as our purpose plan blueprint does not come with us for reference.

We have to figure it out for ourselves.

Some of us know what that fire in our belly is all about. Like we have a lean towards a passion we feel is urgent, one we *must* pursue.

How many of us feel prone not to be pushed into the moulds our parents have planned for us?

Is it therefore mind-blowing to feel free to *be* on the right path where we have a strong instinct of knowing we *are* on it *at last*.

This is despite the scorn of others who are determined to undermine our efforts to succeed.

Is that perhaps their role? Is that perhaps their purpose to put a spanner in the works of certain others? For I guess someone has to play the role. As Shakespeare said:

'All the world's a stage and all the men and women merely players.'

I love it when glimpses occur of what perhaps could be called 'supernatural happenings' therefore that show up in my living of this life. The beings of immense sparkling bright light for instance. They have you feeling so very loved and safe, in their presence. My world then is a beautiful place.

I've had great moments of the highest elations of wonderment — of such amazing happenings that only those who also have experienced for themselves may believe me perhaps. For if not, I wish they too could marvel at such glory where mere words are not enough to describe such happenings. So many for me now to know 'This world is not all there is.'

I once wrote the following:

'I am most grateful for all the beautiful people in my life who have graced it by my knowing them. They stand out like roses amongst the thorns. My love of nature not only gives me joy, but uplifts my entire being just to be in its presence where my spirit soars to marvel at the oneness I feel.'

The highest vibration of love expressed brings peace. I am so grateful when I feel this way, for all else unlike itself is forgotten. I am in awe of how it encapsulates my entire being. I feel absorbed and as one with it, as if I've come home to where I truly belong. I am so grateful to have experienced this.

I feel encouraged to where my journey of learning will finally take me.

Lynette-Kay Lewis

# Keeping the Wolves from My Dreams

Wolves roaming through a shadowy green forest can be very powerful, and intimidating to other small animals, and especially humans. A lone threatening wolf, or worse still, a pack of wolves, if encountered, I would truly avoid their territory. Feeling trapped without support or protection would drive me nuts with anxiety.

Yet one night, safe in my own bed, in my own territory, my dreams were embellished with weird visions of wolves that were enveloping my entire attention. These dreams wouldn't go away. What on earth was happening?

I have referred to myself in the past as *a lone wolf*, being an independent senior citizen. But truly, I'm not lonely. I have family and friends within my very personal journey. Nothing is really changing in my life. So why are my dreams changing, and what are these wolves trying to tell me? A nightmare was emerging in my head with the fear, and the possibility of the risk of injury or death, to me or someone else. The feeling of my energy and control was abruptly diminishing. So unnerving!

It suddenly occurred to me in my dreaming: wolves in the past have a strong association with families. Maybe there was some spiritual meaning or insight to my deep dreaming. Could I be receiving reassurance and a safeguard about the recent changes in my life? Feeling totally secure with the close contact, which I now experience with my loyal family and new trustworthy friends, this had to be the answer. Thanks to the safe wolves in my dreams, I am my accepted sincere self, complete with all my connections.

Kerry Smith

# I'm Free

Into the light of splendour
I come to be eternally blessed.
The dross of my vast shortcomings I've left
Behind now with all of the rest.

I've stepped over the debris
That about me had lain
Of past fears, disappointed hopes,
Nevermore to plague me again.

I've stepped away to leave behind
All fallen hurts from me
To greet the new of dawn
As cleansed I come, to stand tall as a tree.

Refreshed with newness of each breath
From dire and sad forlorn
I stretch my branches to the sky
I feel like I'm reborn.

I'm free of all the dashed of hopes,
of feeling battered and torn
I am feeling now so spry with the frolic of a lamb
I dance and twirl in gleefulness
Of the girl I really am.

Into the light of God's splendour I come
To be eternally blessed
I dance in the light, feeling so sprite
Filled with love spilled to share my best.


Lynette-Kay Lewis.

# The Best Days


The best days are the days
To wake with gratitude
Feeling blessed
To open eyes, look out the window
See the new day dawning

Every day a bonus
Another day to live fully
New experiences, expectations abound
What is on the menu today?
A joyous feeling, what can I taste today?

But of course
Not every day is the best day
There are highs, there are lows
There are times that are hard to bear
Of crushing defeat and weariness

There are tearful days
With no wish to arise
To get up and go
When there is no energy
To greet the day

These are the days of life
A mixture of many ingredients
Some sweet and tasty
Others sour and inedible
What am I to do; why am I here?

But we can make the choice
To make this day the best it can be
One day this day
Will be the last of our life
The day of our final breath

So keep breathing
Enjoy the day this glorious day
With all its sweetness
Its many surprises
Smile and laugh on this day

Join together
In harmony joy and friendship
Make this day the best day
Of your life
In all its richness and diversity

This is not a dress rehearsal
We are acting on the stage of life
In all our costumes, making our speeches
Until we reach the final defining chapter
Of all our days.

Sam Ryan

# The Debris of Life – Space Junk

Life in the fast lane results in debris production and accumulation very quickly. With the advent of space travel and the domination of several countries in this field, the amount of space junk jettisoned into space continues to pile up as it circles the Earth.

Just take for instance, while one report states that there are over two thousand active satellites orbiting Earth, it also says that there are three thousand dead satellites littering space. So we might ask the question: *'How much space junk and debris is circling the Earth?'*

According to NASA, there are one hundred million particles orbiting the Earth, but bear in mind that much of the debris is smaller than a 20-cent piece, and they are even measured in parts of millimetres as they include such things as flecks of paint. NASA estimates that there could be roughly five hundred thousand objects smaller in size than ten centimetres in diameter orbiting Earth.

There are more than twenty-two thousand pieces of junk in space, orbiting Earth that can be seen from the Earth's surface with a telescope or radar. It is estimated that this will increase to fifty-five thousand by the year 2050.

Debris left in orbit below six hundred kilometres will normally fall to Earth within several years. Engineers use the last bits of fuel of spent satellites to slow them down so they will fall out of orbit and burn up in the atmosphere. (spaceplace.nasa.gov). For satellites further away, it takes less fuel to blast them into space than to send them back to Earth.

Quote from this article:

'Perhaps one day in the future, humans may need to send *"space garbage trucks"* to clean these up. But for now, at least, they will be out of the way.'


Robert Nelson

# Life's Observations

Squawking bunch
juicy morsels
fall to the ground.

~ ~ ~

Withered swells
compressed metal plates
mapping futures.

~ ~ ~

Christmas spread
spilt Chinotto
headache in a glass.

Mimma Tornatora

# Life on a Lily Pad

Swaying gently in the breeze
With lightly stirring subtle ease
My mind reflects the tempest past
Was it choice or was it chance?
Maybe, maybe, who's to know
Whether a thing should stay or go?
One does what they know the best
In terms of putting things to rest
Will we ever know the why
Of people aiming for the sky?
Chances are as chances do
So clinging to the mud will rue.

We need to get our gift to fly
In dreams that make the maker cry.
And hope for things that aren't yet dead
So we can fill the space ahead.
Chances are as chances do
Create the facts that fit the shoe.
We will never see the sky
Of hope and dreams if we never try.

Noeline Frost.

# ROMANCE

# The Surfer and the Sea

There's a creature out there in the bay
Who wants to play
She has a tail of green and eyes of blue
And nothing to do
But comb her hair and gaze up at the sky
While a surfer floats by
Feeling the currents and eternal motion
Of the ocean
As the curious creature swirls and curls
The surfer unfurls
Then he slides over the waves and waits
To tempt his fate
Till the creature is possessed with a power
That forms a tower
Rising above them until in a glittering flash
They vanish
Suspended for a second in the sun's glare
Until he escapes her lair
Then the creature retreats to her home in the deep
To whisper and weep
'Come back' as she watches him ride his board
Slowly toward
Distant sands where he turns away from the shore
To go back once more.

Moira Clancy

# To be in Love

Is like a wild ride
Down the rapids
Into swirling eddies
That toss and dance and trill
Into ponds of deeper water
That lie quite still.
There my soul rejoices
For here the pearl is found
Of great price
Where I would sell my possessions
And rest in the harmony
Of God's eternal music.


J. K. Baldock

# Your allure

73

Your allure traps me.
Invocating with those eyes.
I'm lost …
and then …
… found.

Elizabeth Pappas

# Longing

74

Longing for love.
She dreams of Apollo …
but she's married to Zeus.


Elizabeth Pappas

# Eyes

Eyes mesmerizing …
I recognise that gypsy man's look:
it's in my child's eyes.

Elizabeth Pappas

# The Fairy Garden

I see innocence darting
fashioned in lace panties
matching camisole.

I bite my lip
it bleeds
you race to comfort me.

I smell lavender
in your auburn hair
stroke it
pull your face to mine.

I crave the taste of your moist tongue
quickly as a mischievous pixie
you vanish in the canopy.

Your lithe body entices
a game of cat and mouse
I watch you move in the breeze
your nipples ripe.

I yearn to draw you near

  My love
       in
         the
           fairy
             garden.


                Mimma Tornatora

# Woman of Mine

May I watch you while you're sleeping?
May I watch you as you sleep?
Listless now upon your pillow
Happy dreaming from the deep.
In our dreams we live the fancy
Golden butterflies abound
Leaving this dull world we suffer
So take flight to worlds around
Where we ever find our freedom
Freedom of our tales of woe
Ever upward, ever sailing,
On clouds of silver touched with gold
What can we know of dreams untold
Of something way beyond.
May I watch you while you're sleeping?
Woman of mine
Let the dreamtime roll.

J. K. Baldock

# TRAVEL

# The Monitor

We had been in Hawaii a week, on Oahu. We had a great time, but now it was time to go home.

We had boarded the Qantas 747 and sat in our allocated seats, 52B and 52C. People continued to board until all were seated. The engines started, and we sat waiting for the Flight Attendants to do their thing, when I said to my husband:

'Listen to that engine on our right. It sounds odd.'

He listened, and remarked: 'Yes, you're right. It does sound odd.'

'What should we do?' I said. 'Put up our hand and say "Excuse me. Your engine sounds off?"'

He said: 'Surely they have some sort of monitor to tell them if their engines are functioning properly?'

'I guess they must,' I said, unconvinced, but lacking the confidence to show 'my ignorance.'

We concluded that they must surely be in control, and sat with our fingers crossed.

All the usual announcements were made, and we set off down the runway in preparation for take-off. The plane seemed to ascend successfully, and we began to relax.

After a few minutes, the captain announced that there was a fault in one of the engines, and we would have to return to Honolulu. However, it would be impossible to land with such a full load of fuel, so we would have to circle for three hours to jettison some of it.

Following those three hours, we had to sit on the plane for a further five hours while the engineers tried to discern the problem, and attempted to deal with it. We were then told we would have to leave the plane and be put up in hotels overnight while a Rolls Royce engine was shipped out of Sydney.

Good grief! Everyone's plans of connecting flights, being collected by relatives, etc., etc., were on the rocks. We had been scheduled to meet friends in Sydney, and spend a nice afternoon with them and John Waters' mum. Disappointing to have to miss out. Also, our children were expecting us home the next day. What a pain.

The conditions in the cabin were steadily becoming more unpleasant, as the cabin crew reckoned they had completed their shift, so they sat and ignored the needs of all the passengers. It was not a pretty sight!

After what seemed like an eternity, the captain announced that the engine fault was because the fibreglass lining of the engine was coming adrift, so they had decided they would just rip it out, and go without it. There were many worried faces around the plane, however, we took off again, and without mishap, covered the distance between Honolulu and Sydney in one piece. A round of applause heralded our landing. What a relief.

How odd that I was the only one to notice the strange noise of the engine.

I must have been the only effective monitor they had, but unfortunately, in this instance, the sound was turned off!

P. J. Mistilis

# Pappouli

A heroic chip off the old Hellenic block is Eleni's *Pappouli*
Leaning in curved arthritic repose,
having gently navigated in unison,
his long-bent legs
into the *creaking* of a reed strung chair.

He flips smooth worry beads to an unrelenting rhythmic
*click, click, click* …
a timepiece … beloved stringy adult soothers,
a gift from his dying father …
when he was a boy, and now …
having wooed away at least two lifetimes of
uncertainties and loss, they endure, marking time.

Eventually, the '*tut*' of '*oxi*'
expressed with a quick elevation of the chin.
He declines the old soldier,
the ticket hawker's exaggerated routine appeal.
And sips coffee, savoring in long *slurps,*
recollections in exotic notes …
from the long-gone hashish dens of Piraeus.
Radio rebetiko *thumps* as punters play,
intent on the roll and *tap* of *tavli* dice.

*Pappouli's* sanctuary …
amid flareups of *yelling* from philosophers and fools alike.
Attuning his intellect to the day's anarchists on stage …
amid the intonations at Spiro's *kafeneio*.
He drifts in and out of rehashed, hot, simmering debates …
such therapy.
Welcome diversions from those dim and dispersed pauses …
brutal punctuations plaguing his ever-shortening days.


Elizabeth Pappas

# I Want Not to Hear

I want not to hear the wailing of the refugee mothers …
Piercing the winds sweeping across my Greek island home.
A place where ice-cube-fashioned villas line horseshoe-shaped
bays.
And pink bougainvillea blossoms smile all summer long.
But there, lining the *limani* are the rows of tiny pale coffins.
Cold in baking sun, sleeping babes in hushed spectral mirages.
That prowl … seeping into snowy walls,
pairing with the white shutters
of small shot-back eyes …
Oh, how I want not to hear the wailing of the refugee mothers…
But … pleading … my pleading … lodges nowhere.


Elizabeth Pappas

# The Turkish Cleric

The Turkish cleric smiles smugly.
Behind his legislation.
Lubing his edgy palms.
Come in … suckers.

Elizabeth Pappas

# Risotto Maestro

87

Risotto Maestro.
It's Dolce and Gabbana served on a plate.
Subsumed, I launch into Italy.


Elizabeth Pappas

# DRAMA

# **Death Wrings Out**

Death wrings out the refugees like laundry into orderly lines.
Then all too soon white flannelled Greek sailors,
mute like grieving fathers,
carry in procession tiny pale coffins to customs.
One young sailor, overcome … soils his front.
His eyes into mine and I weep …
I weep as if they are all my children.


Elizabeth Pappas

# Shackle Me

92

Shackle me to the ledge.
Of the cliff of my love's slip.
A hangman ... my new man.
Our first date ...
My last ...

Elizabeth Pappas

# **Poppy Day**

93

Anzac skewered, pinned like a butterfly specimen.
Mute on a stranger's lapel.
Scarlet, petal-shaped wings, black opiate heart …
And still, there's no balm to soothe and heal those seams of loss.
No settling stillness, or ease into peace.
Only silent cries, 'He's paid your bloody butcher's bill.'

Elizabeth Pappas

# Some Sort of Tragedy

Summer stretches into February here,
And I never get used to it –

That when November ends
Life will not lull into
A fog.
That the day will not end at four,
That we will not curl up by the kerosene heater
And wait for the wavering sun
That we are not propped figures
peeling oranges and peanuts
Looking at the pastel globe
A shell of herself –
Quietly.
Quickly
descend behind the jagged buildings.

January is the cold month my father was born
He is still and
Stoic like the juniper tree.
We gift him mittens and mufflers
hold onto the sleeves of his coat
As if it will protect us from some sort of
Tragedy that winter brings.

December is
saying goodbye to my friends wrapped in scarves and
Blazers that were much too wide for our heads
We would return in spring
A little bit taller,
A little bit older
So we started fitting our clothes much better.

When November ends
We do not pack lights
And seal them in a box until next year
The marigolds will not come down from our doors
With the purple amaranth globes.
Fruits and nuts in the prayer room
Will not slowly start to mould
The sky will wax to a bright orange and purple
Descend on the city, sticky with heat.

Summer will stretch into February,
And I never get used to it.

Kritika Lama

# The Gift

96

Gift from Mommy.
Candy pink cake and an *emasculation* for his sixteenth
You say: *'Body modification.'*
I say: *'Genital mutilation.'*
'You say … I say … let's call the whole thing off.'

Elizabeth Pappas

# The Letter

He sat at his beautifully crafted oak desk. He was in emotional turmoil, head in his hands, heart racing, feeling as though his scalp was going to lift off and disperse all the contents of his brain. He was in despair, a sense of agitation overtaking him. What to do for the best – the best for him. That was his priority. It was mostly always about him and his needs; that was how he had lived his adult life up until now. He did not think that selfish, simply self-preservation.

The letter lay on the desk, blinking sightlessly at him, drawing him back to its contents. Unwillingly, his eyes kept going back to it; he definitely didn't want to read it again but it was a letter that demanded his attention, and very soon.

He leaned back in a very comfortable black leather chair, swivelled it around, and looked out through the open French doors to the very green, lush tropical garden, hoping for some release from this feeling of tension, the blinding headache that was now developing behind his eyes.

During the years of much hard work, he had made a good life with no attachments to the past; he had been, and continued to be, very successful in the industry he was so passionate about and he knew from feedback that he was much admired and respected by all and sundry. His credentials and credibility in the business world were well established and intact. He had moved around from State to State as his job prospects grew; he had climbed the ladder of increasing success and was now enjoying the very comfortable lifestyle he had always sought.

Professionally he was at the top of his game; he bathed in the glow of deep satisfaction from all that he had achieved and with all the plaudits that he had received over the years. His talents, abilities and knowledge recognised, he was seen to be a leader in his field of endeavour. He had created an image of himself that was far removed from his beginnings.

He had lived his life on his terms, a man in control of his destiny. He had re-imagined and re-told his life story in a way that had little or no connection to the past. Up until now it had all worked so well; he was a proud man, no doubt arrogant and dismissive at times, brooking no argument, no sign of a chink in his armour, firm in the decisions he had made, both professional and personal.

This letter had arrived out of the blue; in recent years he had rarely received any mail by regular post. How had it found him? In this high-tech world of the internet and social media, and despite the fact that he was well-known, he had managed over the years to keep his private life very private indeed. The correct address was on the envelope and, when he first opened it, there was no hint or suggestion that the life he had carved out for himself was about to change. Forever. Or would it?

What could he do to make all this go away? What strategies could he put in place so that he didn't have to face the contents of this uninvited letter? So that no action was demanded of him? His brain was buzzing with all sorts of ideas of how he could make all this go away. The headache was increasingly worse; it was now thumping, and he was starting to feel nauseous.

He stood up and walked out into the garden, hoping for some relief. It was a warm slightly humid day; the automated sprinklers had been on and the leaves and vibrant tropical blooms glistened in the very bright sunshine. Beautiful, but not very good for a crushing headache, he thought. The garden had always given him much pleasure, but not today.

He was spinning; feeling out of control was disturbing and debilitating and his agitation was increasing. Something had to be done, but what? He felt exhausted just thinking about all the possible actions he could take to relieve his current anxiety. He certainly did not want a can of worms to be opened, for all his secrets, his hidden life, to fly out of Pandora's Box. The image he had created was very important for his sense of self and well-being, of always being in control. He had become the image. He did not want or seek any form of public scrutiny.

He was feeling nervous, edgy, like being on a tightrope; something he had not felt for a very long time. Maybe he should go for a dip in the pool, shimmering blue and inviting in the sunshine. But he didn't have the energy for that either. He felt immobilised, stuck to the spot. Usually, he was decisive even when faced with challenges, of which he'd had a few in his life. But today was different; this letter had delivered a very real body blow that was in danger of knocking him off his feet and plunging him into a deep dark well of uncertainty and a huge feeling of helplessness. He needed to get back that feeling of power, to feel in control once again.

He shook his head in despair and walked back inside to his study. It was a beautiful room that he had created to be a peaceful sanctuary, with mellow floor-to-ceiling oak shelving to house his specialty books; a very workable space, light and airy, a joy to be in every day. His Retreat, everything at his fingertips. Why did it now feel so cold? The breeze coming through the open doors from the garden was warm, inviting and aromatic, but he felt shivers running up and down his spine. He shuddered to try and ease the feeling but, within himself, he felt as cold as the room.

The letter on the desk beckoned; he could screw it up and throw it in the bin, or even shred it, but that would not make the contents go away now that he had read them. The words were in his head, he could not make them disappear. He did not like what was happening, he had his life planned out; he knew where he was going and where he wanted to be. This letter and its contents were not part of the plan.

It was not a very long letter. Written on expensive cream paper, it had an elegant letterhead, but the contents were demanding action which he did not wish to take. It seemed obvious at this point that he would have little choice but to respond. But was there another way to deal with this? He left the letter on the desk and walked out of the study. This letter he could not deal with today, maybe tomorrow would be a better day once he could map out overnight his strategy of how to respond.

His sleep was elusive with much tossing and turning during the night; the next morning he felt no closer to achieving a permanent solution to this unsettling dilemma, and his headache continued to rage. Life was presenting him with a deeply personal challenge, and he felt like a lost child once again, swept along on a tide of change not of his making.

He had no wish to return to the past, and he was going to make sure he did not return. He was firmly determined about that. It was now late afternoon and he had finally decided that he would turn over this page and start another chapter, regardless of the consequences. This then was his latest strategy. It had always worked in the past. The shredder was beside the desk, the letter in his hand.


Sam Ryan

# The Bag Lady

In the park is a shelter of trees,
Starlit in the dark, blankets of leaves,
Far away from the stares of those
Who reside here in the cool shadows
With gardens of lavender and roses
High heels and takeaway meals
Church bells that ring on Sundays
Now I sleep on street corners where
Hooded figures are doing deals
While the congregations gather
To sing hymns and give sermons
About the new day that's on the way.

Moira Clancy

# The Dance of Our Life

We stand in total darkness. There's just enough space for two couples to squeeze behind the folded side curtain. My bosom is about to explode with fright. My knees feel like buckling underneath me. I must take hold of myself. 'Breathe deeply!' I coax myself.

Suddenly a buzz emerges from the other side, inflating with laughter and chatter. More deep breathing, stretching, and flexing of legs. The wait becomes intolerable. Without notice, the countdown starts from behind us. The music erupts. The thick curtain of the small Playhouse Theatre goes up slowly revealing the colourful backdrop of La Boca-Buenos Aires-Argentina in the fifties. The adrenalin kicks in while the cast and crew are set on autopilot mode.

The first European migrants make their entrance on the streets of Argentina. In no time I'm whisked on stage, thrown into the folkloric Chamamé dance – the essence of the present traditional Argentine Tango. After the first few steps, I feel more relaxed and can enjoy the dance and vibrant energy coming from the other two couples.

Soon we bow and exit to resounding applause. Our bodies filled with buoyancy and excitement, we bounce backstage for a two-minute change ready for another scene and dance, with everyone lending a helping hand along the way. The spectators are entertained non-stop for two hours, with a change of décor, dance, music and singing, narrating the history of Argentine Tango. All members of the troop, after a long year of intense practice, exceeding their wildest dream, give out the best of themselves to the audience. My childhood dream was becoming a reality at the most unexpected time of my life.

As a little girl, I always loved dancing. It was for me a natural expression of joy, pirouetting in front of the mirror, moving to the rhythm of music. Embedded deeply in my being was a nascent little pearl – the desire to dance. This little pearl remained hidden for years, as, on my way home from school, I watched other more fortunate little girls taking their dance lessons. When television made its appearance in our house, waltzes took my soul and senses fleeting through the room. A broom became the ideal partner as we careered around the polished floor of the dining room.

Migrating to Australia in the late 70's was a blessing. It was the land of all possibilities! I realised it wasn't too late to learn dancing, amongst other things. Fortunately for me, my husband Cecil was very amenable to trying his two left feet on the dance floor. It was a slow, rewarding process. Social ballroom trained us through the realm of specific routines for men and women. Keen and committed, we both were, going home and practicing every move in our family room. Like children, we would show off our new skills to friends and family members. The waltz enticed us with its more gentle, soft flowing rhythm until we discovered the Argentine Tango.

This dance impelled us into a whirlwind of cultural surprises and emotions. Cecil was enthralled by it from the onset. True to the Latin machismo, the men were taught how to lead and the women how to follow. Nearly an impossible task at first, coming from ballroom training where posture is very different, and routines are learned. Two years from our initial taste of the Argentine Tango, we were under the spell of this dance which emerged as a desire on my part to discover Latin dances. For many years, we were kept unravelling the intricacies, complexities and intrigues of a dance encultured in a nation full of contrasts.

Our eagerness to learn the dance brought us to partake in the Argentine instructor's vision and dream. An incredible buzz permeated our life during the years 2000-2001. To promote the show, we were called upon to give street performances in some of the Australian cities — namely Perth, Bunbury, Albany, Brisbane, and Canberra. We danced in cafés and on top of raised catwalks in the middle of major shopping centres; were photographed for community papers; wrote articles; did television advertising. Overnight, we became dancers, advertisers, costume producers, stage assistants, to name just a few tasks. Adults of various age groups, professions, and trades were united in devoting evenings and weekends for a yearlong extraordinary adventure.

The Argentine Tango Show became the catalyst for many of us to realise and achieve some locked-away dreams. Involvement in it took on a different meaning for each of us. Performing on stage catapulted me into sheer gripping panic followed by an unbelievable adrenalin boost propelling me beyond my inner insecurities. A moment of inconceivable freedom! Utterly unfathomable at this stage of our lives to be treated like stars with bouquets of flowers delivered to our glittering dressing room by our son and his girlfriend.

The two-hour showcase of historical Tango Dance closed in Perth, after a matinée and two consecutive nights, with a vibrant array of elaborate tango costumes, with dancers sashaying on stage depicting various styles of tango dancing to the famous Piazzola music – *La Cumparsita* – a perfect finale for cast and crew linked by an indescribable bond of achievement and inner success. Tears of joy welled in my eyes as I stepped forward to meet Cecil from the opposite side of the stage to bow to the audience. We were overwhelmed with emotion and pure exhilaration, being applauded by our children, family members and friends in the audience.

As the curtain dropped to wild applause, a new venture had just sprung up in our lives. Other Australian cities awaited us. It was an uplifting, bewildering experience for the soul, that only a sense of vision and dream could accomplish. We did it! A testimony to the future generations of our family that it's never too late to reach one's full potential, to live out a dream, to learn new skills. The curtain of our life remained lifted high from that moment onwards, to new dreams and possibilities.


Marie-Anne Pontré

# A Woman, a Hubby, an Aunt and a Dance

The woman walked into the room – a modest and intimate dining room. Susan was her name, a sixties-something mother and grandmother, an empty nester, happily married to George, both retired, living the life. The ambient amber glow of two candles burning on the perfectly laid table for two filled the room with a delicate perfume. Susan smiled sweetly as she sniffed the soft, scintillating air. A bottle of red wine breathed as two empty glasses stood yearning for fulfilment.

She heard a knock at the door.

'I'll get it!' she yelled into an ocean of silence. She answered it. A delivery driver stood quietly, holding a huge package. Susan looked puzzled as she signed for it. As she walked back into the dining room with the puzzling package, George burst out from the kitchen, dressed in a Spanish dance costume, proclaiming in the worst attempt at a Spanish accent:

'Bon Jour, Senyalita!'

Susan shook her head in disbelief, proclaiming back, 'Bon Jour is French, George, not Spanish, and it's Senorita, not Senyalita.'

George replied, a little incensed, 'Just trying to get in the mood, Darl.'

He spotted the package, 'Oh good, I see you got my pressie', he said. 'Well, go on, open it.'

Susan reluctantly opened the package, to reveal a Spanish dance dress. She shook it out. She took a rose from a vase. A vase made for two and only two. Two exactly perfect roses, uniform, exactly the same in every way. She held the rose in full view of George, and questioned him. 'You don't honestly expect me to put this in my mouth, do you?'

George could not contain his enthusiasm as he cheerfully answered, 'Don't worry, they're not real.'

Susan dumped the rose back in the vase as George hurried away from the dining room, proclaiming, 'You're grumpy because you're hungry; back in a sec. You can pour the wine, it's breathed.'

She poured two glasses of wine. George returned, almost in an instant, with a piping hot dish of paella, and placed it triumphantly in the middle of the table.

'Ta da!' George declared excitedly.

Susan shook her head, trying not to seem ungrateful, but he could sense something.

'What's the matter?' George asked. 'I thought paella was your favourite.'

'It is,' answered Susan, 'but not every night for the past two weeks.'

'It's Spanish,' replied George. 'Get us in the mood.'

Susan slumped on the table. She sighed in bafflement as her head cascaded into the well of her folded arms. Gently, with his right index finger, George raised her chin. Their eyes met in a knowingness of long-time love. As he smiled gently, she begged the question, 'Honestly, George, who in God's Universe not only insists on a Spanish-themed birthday party, but wants all the guests to learn the Flamenco, too?' Susan asked.

George tenderly replied, 'Your 101-year-old Aunty, that's who.'

'Three days' time, George. 101 in three days' time,' she replied.

'Come on, love,' George sympathetically retorted. 'You know her lifetime dream was to go to Spain.'

'Yes, I know, and I've only heard that story like a gazillion times over the years. What I can't understand is why she never did. She could have easily afforded it,' replied Susan.

Susan now reflected on a child's memory of a long time past. 'You know she used to have this tiny set of castanets when I was little. I don't know where they got to. She would click them briefly as she exited after her visits. I loved that.'

George rubbed his hands together in glee. 'Well then, we'd better not waste any more time. We've only got three days to get it right. Eat, then dance,' he said as he pulled Susan's chair out for her.

A little later, now in their lounge room, Susan and George, both dressed in their cheesy Spanish Dance costumes, were rearranging the furniture to create a dance floor. George grabbed a DVD and held it up for Susan to acknowledge its title, *Spanish Dancing for Idiots*. Susan giggled as George settled the DVD into its rhythm. He then took one of the roses from the vase, which was now on the coffee table, and on grinning the biggest grin he could manage, threw it between his teeth. He handed Susan the other rose. She took it, then promptly threw it back into the vase and shook her head. On his obvious reluctant acceptance of her reaction, he put his arms up, ready for dancing.

Susan took up her position. Concentration was rife on the musical image emanating from the flat screen. One first step by both of them. Bang! Noses bounced like two balloons in a game at a child's birthday party. Shock, then upturned mouths, a little chuckle at first, dissolving into uncontrollable, uncontained laughter.

Susan's mobile rang. George laughingly glanced across at the number. 'It's your sister.' Susan grabbed the phone, still in her jovial stupor. 'I'll be quick; she's probably just ringing to see if we still want the frangipani,' she said.

Susan answered, giggling, 'Hi Jen, yep we will take the frangipan …'

Susan's voice stopped, dead. Her sparkling laughing eyes slowly turned to fluid pools of anguish. Tears ran down her face. Her blurry gaze glued to George's. A momentary lapse in concentration, as disbelief set in. Her focus darted back to the phone.

'Yep, you can't talk for long, you have to do the ring around. I understand. Thanks for letting me know. At least she got her telegram from the Queen. Love you.'

Susan pressed the little red hang-up dot on her iPhone. She fell into George's embrace, sobbing. 'She just fell asleep and didn't wake up.'

George hugged Susan tight. They took a moment. But then, Susan suddenly broke away, her fluid eyes now dry with determination. With great gusto, she grabbed her dumped rose from the vase and exclaimed, 'Let's do her proud.'

With a sweeping wave of theatrics, Susan clenched the rose between her welcoming teeth. George picked up the remote, and masterfully restarted the DVD. They took their positions, looking all the part for real this time. Eyes glued at first to the screen, then to each other, as they mastered the Flamenco. A little later and dance in full swing, the DVD stopped of its own accord. A confused glance between the two lovers as a swish of air rushed over their heads. A quick click of castanets rattled from the Cosmos.

They both giggled as the DVD restarted, again of its own accord.

And with full-blown laughter, they continued like there was no tomorrow.


Lacey Healey

# Her Name was Phyllis.

I close my eyes and see my mother walking in front of me. A woman of voluptuous proportions, not like me, a skinny child. She is brave too, and I'm a bit nervous as it's getting dark and the buildings around us are grey and glistening with damp. It must have rained before we arrived, and it looks creepy. We walk past a pub and a wave of noise and chattering voices comes and goes in the gloom as we carry on walking. Mum knows where she's going but I don't. All I know is that she was born around here. This is her town but not mine. It's the place where Jack the Ripper once lurked down dark alleyways, like the one we've just passed. Suddenly we duck into a doorway and Mum opens a door into a room full of people. I smell food, not the type of food they serve at the school canteen, but Mum's kind of food.

She knows everyone here, does my mother. There are rows of tables full of people. Mum's sort of people, and she stops and talks to someone at every table. We finally sit down at the back of the restaurant. It's called the 'Old Friends' and the manageress looks like Mum. They could be related, but they don't really know if they are. What they do know is that they are friends with much in common. Anyway, I'm relieved when we sit down, as old ladies we pass keep pinching me and they say: 'Is she yours, Phyllis?'

And Mum says 'Yes'.

'She no look like you,' they reply, and give me a funny look. By the time we sit down, I'm beginning to wonder if this woman I live with really is my mum. She doesn't seem to have any doubts, so I keep this thought to myself. After all, where would

I be without her? Not here in this restaurant, that's for sure.

I know my mum is different from the other mums where I come from, and mostly in a good way, as we go to lots of places. Some of my friends have never even been to London, but I go every week as Mum can't buy the food she eats in Northampton, where I was born. Things like spices, that my friends have never heard of, and garlic. We get those in Gerard Street. Then we have afternoon tea at the Ritz and usually catch the train home, but we didn't do that today. We came here to the East End for dinner instead. I've been here before, by taxi, but this is the first time we've used the tube and walked down these old streets that are still surrounded by bomb sites. I felt that this was a place I wouldn't like to be if I was walking here on my own.

Mum was born in these parts in 1925 at 34 Pennyfields, to be precise, a street near the docks in Limehouse, Poplar, London E.14. People born there have a wide variety of backgrounds but regardless of what they look like, they are all cockneys.

When the Second World War commenced in 1939 the whole area around the Limehouse Causeway and the street called Pennyfields was known as 'China Town'. It was a place that provided well for the Asian sailors working the Oriental routes into the Port of London. The main attractions for these men, back then, were the opium dens, hidden behind the shops in Limehouse and Poplar, as well as the availability of prostitutes, along with Chinese grocers, restaurants, and seamen's lodging houses. These things attracted all sorts of people as well as the oriental sailors. For example, it was a well-known haunt of the aristocracy who liked nothing more than 'slumming it' for an evening of entertainment in the many pubs, bars, and nightclubs.

In other words, if you were born in Limehouse you weren't always sure of your parentage. My mother, however, had a birth certificate. Stamped across it in red was the word 'Illegitimate'. She spent her life being ashamed of that birth certificate and was reluctant to show it to anyone unless absolutely necessary. I only saw it when I was eighteen and signed the registry when she married for the second time. Then I stared at it for as long as seemed polite, knowing that I might never get another chance and I memorised my maternal grandmother's name, which was Mary Euphemia Thompson, born in Cardiff. My maternal grandfather's name was Yong Tan-Kow, a ship's carpenter, born in Shanghai. Apart from their names, I have no idea what their story was; it could have been a love story or a simple business arrangement. Who would know, but my guess is that my grandmother was in the 'entertainment business'. The thing is, though, my mother and her two sisters were raised in care, survived their childhoods, then a war, and after that lived good lives before passing away in old age. I salute them all.

Finally, I wish to record that Mum was the bravest woman I've ever known. The only thing that ever frightened her, as far as I could tell, was showing that birth certificate to anyone.

As a child, and young woman, there were many things that frightened me, but I knew the value of knowing with certainty who I was, and being able to show my birth certificate to anyone without feeling any fear or embarrassment. My family background and the career I've had in justice and child protection has also shown me the full value of this simple thing in life that we take for granted.


Moira Clancy

# Bearing Witness

He and his little brother had only just visited her on Saturday. After walking about two miles up the hill from their home to the tram stop, they caught the tram to Stone's Corner, which was just near the hospital. Her sons were only ten and thirteen; both were tall, handsome and athletic lads. The older boy was extremely independent and was constantly acting in loci parentis to his younger sibling, whenever their mother was in hospital and their father was away on the Gold Coast.

They were looking forward to seeing their mother. The hospital ward was sterile, cold, clinical, and unwelcoming. Their mother was in a curtained cubicle, her wheezing easily heard as the boys arrived at the door of the ward. The wheezing was a familiar sound, like a wet sponge being squeezed out. They came in; she smiled broadly and motioned to them to sit on her bed, one on each side. She reached out to hold each boy's hand. Her breathing laboured away in between holding the oxygen mask to her face and taking in deep breaths. She managed to ask questions about school, their friends and Mrs Farmer's cooking. She loved to hear their stories and they laughed and giggled as they joked about some of the awful meals Mrs Farmer prepared. May was always shattered by these visits, but she adored her boys and loved every minute of their time together. Their visits were happy times in extremely difficult circumstances.

The Matron at Mater Hospital was an authoritative, stiff and imposing figure, who oversaw patient care and all the nurses. She had such a ferocious look that one might think that she would eat her young. Her Matron's cap, her starched collar, cuffs and her crisp white uniform signalled that she was in charge and what she said was to happen, always did happen!

The Matron stood at the door after the young visitors had been with their mother for about twenty minutes. She told them that their mum was improving and that she would be coming home soon. She instructed them that it was best not to stay too long, as their mum, May, found it exhausting and needed her rest. The boys reluctantly left to catch the rattling, old green and yellow tram home, feeling reassured that it would not be long before their lives would return to normal, and their mum would be home.

That night their mother passed away; she suffered a massive heart attack and could not be revived.

In the 40s and 50s, treatments and prevention options for asthma sufferers were limited. May did use a personal inhaler, which allowed her to breathe aerosols generated by epinephrine. The symptoms were thought to be brought on by emotional conditions and elevated levels of stress. Little research had been done to identify environmental allergens and other triggers.

May was a chronic asthmatic, having suffered from debilitating symptoms since she was a child. She always had a cough, a rattling wheeze and was continually gasping for air. As a little girl she was encouraged to swim, play tennis and dance. She loved these activities and became quite accomplished at all three. These highly aerobic pursuits were considered to help with opening the airways and assisting the asthmatic to breathe more freely. She often felt energized and more alive when she was involved in physical pursuits.

During her lifetime, May experienced many extended stays in the Mater Hospital. She was often admitted suffering from pneumonia and chronic bronchitis. The treatment on so many occasions involved the use of adrenergic bronchodilator injections which left her arms and thighs covered in unsightly black and blue bruises. Despite the limitations placed on her by her medical condition, she endeavoured to live a rich and active life.

May was brought up in a committed Christian family. They worshipped together and were highly active within the Anglican Church. When May started working, she was offered the role of Assistant to the Archbishop of Brisbane. She travelled to Africa on the Guinea Coast as a missionary with the Worldwide Evangelistic Crusade and formed a strong relationship with Mable, another much older missionary. Later, upon her return to Australia, May was introduced to Ernest, Mable's son. He and May were involved in the preparation of debutantes on behalf of the Archdiocese of Brisbane. They taught the young women to dance, curtsey, follow etiquette and to learn all the subtleties of the art of social networking. This was all for the formal coming out of the young women and their introduction to society.

Ernest was considered the black sheep of his family and his behaviours – drinking, smoking, and womanizing – were a complete affront to his family, as they too, were committed Christians. He rejected the bible teachings of his childhood and preferred a life of indulgence and excess. He hadn't admitted his alcohol-fuelled violent behaviour to anyone, not even himself.

It did not take long for May and Ernest to become an item, enjoying playing tennis at the Community Tennis Club and swimming at the Lang Baths. She was completely captivated by his bad-boy image and devil-may-care attitude to life. They married in 1949 and welcomed two sons in the first few years of marriage. May was a wonderful mother and was always cooking the boys' favourites: homemade crumpets, toffee apples and marshmallows. Friday nights were always special because Ernest often did not come home on weekends. May observed the

Christian tradition of no meat on Fridays. Dinner was always South African fillet and homemade chips wrapped in newspaper cones for her boys. Fridays were a precious time for both May and her children.

Over the next few years, the relationship between May and Ernest soured, indeed, curdled. May immersed herself in the raising of her sons, her night shift at the International Telephone Exchange and her charity work. Ernest pursued his life of excess away from his family, never spending any real quality time being a father and husband.

A few weeks before May was hospitalised this time, Ernest had arrived home drunk and belligerent; he was looking for a fight and May was always his target. His anger was palpable; he had a mean, violent streak. He had been away for a few weeks, spending time with his girlfriend. His family ran a bad last when it came to his obsession with Marlene, a glamorous married woman with whom he had been fascinated since well before he met and married May. With Marlene, he was able to slosh down whiskey, listen to all the crooning jazz singers and pretend to himself that he didn't have any family responsibilities.

A blazing row began with him criticizing May, calling her names, belittling her, picking on her boys, and accusing her of running around with other men. She held her tongue for a long time until he began to push her around. He grabbed her by the arm.

She screamed: 'Ernest, please, you are hurting me.'

His fingers were digging into her arm.

'Please, the boys are frightened.'

'I cannot breathe, please stop!'

He struck her across the face, grabbed her by the neck and shoved her against the wall. She screeched like a wounded animal.

He let her go; she slumped to the floor gasping like bellows, and wheezing. Screaming and begging him to stop served only to infuriate him more. The scene was always the same, straight from the abuser's playbook. It played out over and over every time he returned to Holland Park from the Gold Coast.

That night he had gone too far. Her fragile frame was slumped on the floor. May couldn't breathe, her lips were blue, her breaths were shallow. Ernest panicked and screamed to their oldest son, who was a terrified witness, to get her atomizer from the bathroom cabinet. Frantic, she took some huge puffs, but it was too difficult to breathe. Ernest called 000 and the ambulance arrived, sirens blaring with red lights flashing. Oxygen was administered and an adrenalin injection was given. Her boys watched from the porch as their mother was once again taken away to hospital for who knew how long.

Her asthma was severe and difficult to stabilize. May developed pneumonia again which meant a long stay so she could be treated with antibiotics and, of course, constant adrenalin injections. It was an extended stay this time, as she struggled to regain her strength and her good health.

The boys had only been at home for a few hours after their Saturday visit to see May.

The police arrived at the family home around seven-thirty in the evening and informed them of her death. Her eldest son stood in the passageway, for what seemed like an eternity. Hearing his beautiful mother being spoken about in the past tense made him feel sick. He was overwhelmed with grief. He began to sob uncontrollably, primal gut-wrenching sobs.

What was going to happen? The complete chaos of their lives was laid bare.

The hardest part of losing his mother was the constant tense correction. It was a cruel reminder that what was once so real would just now be memories. All that was to be her life would be unlived and not shared with her boys. They had witnessed such heartless and brutish treatment of their wonderful mother, her constant struggle with a debilitating disease and her indominable spirit and now she was gone.


Helen Pears

# Under the Breath of a Moonlit Night

Stealthily, under the cover of darkness, he opens his front door, steps outside and closes the door behind him. He proceeds to his car and silently opens the door. He slides in behind the steering wheel and drives as quietly as possible to the outskirts of town, turning northwards to bushland.

He quickly gets out and opens the boot to get wooden pegs, a hammer, and a torch, and walks into the bush. He locates a peg, then places one of his pegs, corner to corner, and hammers it into the ground. He then locates another three pegs and repeats the process so that his pegs are just inside those other pegs marking out a mining lease.

He then gets into his car and drives to Perth, parking his car in the Mines Department parking lot so he can be first at the Mining Registrar's office come opening time. As the Mines Department office opens, he steps inside and goes directly to the office counter to lay his claim to this mining lease which was two inches inside the pegs placed by the mining company who had made this claim before him. He had discovered that their lease was due to expire at midnight the day before, so took the opportunity to lay his claim before the other party renewed their lease. When *they* arrived at the Mining Registrar's office, they could only claim the two inches around the outside, which they did.

In his car, he heads back to his town and to his job as a barber, as if nothing was amiss.

Over the coming months, locals are recruited, work starts on the mine site and the infrastructure starts to take shape. The office and all the structures relating to the running of the mine, the working structures as in conveyor belt, and tanks for sluicing and separating the gold from the other materials are built, as are the smelting sheds and gold pouring area to produce the bars of gold ready for sale.

The production started, and on the day of the first pour, the mine owners invited many people out to watch. The first bar was about half the size of a loaf of bread and was worth close to $35,000.

Luckily for me, I worked for Telstra and helped put the phones into the mine. The boss of the mine lived next door to me, so I had two invitations to the day in question, one from Don, the next-door neighbour, and one via Telstra, for us to attend.

We watched the bar of gold being passed around. I did not get to handle it, but many others did. It weighed sixteen kilograms, and as I previously said, it was worth *thirty-five thousand dollars!*

Yes, this seemingly far-fetched story did actually happen in Southern Cross in the years of 1987, 1988 and 1989. The mine was in operation for many years, and it all began under the breath of a moonlit night.

As far as I know, the barber is no longer barbering.


Robert Nelson

# NATURE
## and the
# ENVIRONMENT

# I Have a Bee in My Bonnet

I have a bee in my bonnet that buzzes all day
The noise and obsession will not go away.
Even when going to bed at night
I know that there's something not quite right.

I'm concerned by my worry about true bees in my head
Not the bee phobia that others can dread.
Without real bees we would not be alive
As humans, we need them on earth to survive.

Pollinating the plants and the fruit that we eat
Providing us with honey that's healthy and sweet.
Bee pollen, a superfood, is a natural essential
Packed with nutrients and antioxidants that are fundamental.

Never take for granted the state of the bees
Now impacted by climate change, fires, and fewer trees.
We have to find a way to make a difference
To ensure the bees are in our future existence.

This concept in my mind is how important bees are
And not just for the honey we buy in a jar.
Protecting the bees must be our focused fixation
Free the buzzing from our bonnets, and ease the situation.

Kerry Smith

# I Wander

124

I wander the beach.
Heron steps upon the damp sand.
Inhibitions unclenched, I toss a call into the sky:
'Please come dance with me …'


Elizabeth Pappas

# Land of Mine

Land of mine, land of mine
Where is your beauty?
Rich red furrows that furrow your brow
Then the green trees, red gum and white,
Then the flowers as pure as light,
What of the wind that speaks through the leaves?
Land of mine when I die,
Embraced by your bosom,
Earth Mother I cry,
Land of mine, land of mine
Tell me your starting, your growing, your end,
Together, together, both of us dancing!
Ever the dance, the dance to the end.

J.K. Baldock

# A Winter's Night

You announced you were coming in late afternoon
When grey clouds appeared in the distance
As they moved ever closer the darker they became
An atmosphere of pending foreboding.

Galahs in their numbers fly overhead
Screeching as they pass
Hurrying back home to their cosy nests
Before the storm erupts.

Then comes the wind, howling and whistling
Blowing the last autumn leaves from the trees
A flurry of those that had already fallen
Are whipped up and left piled by the kerb.

Darkness falls and the display begins
Shimmering sheets of white light up the distant sky
Closer, forked lightning's brilliance blazes earthwards
Illuminating the darkness and spectacular to the eye.

A brief pause is all it takes before thunderclaps rend the air
Like mighty cannons they roll overhead
Rumbling and booming with power and might
Oh, my goodness, I'm so glad I'm tucked up warm tonight.

This heavenly game is brought to a halt
As rain spills out of the clouds
Pelting down on the countryside
Upon the homes beneath.

From this display of might and power
Many times our world is graced
By a rainbow of many colours
And a return to a world of peace.

Dorothy Littmann

# Dusk's Salmon Quilt

Dusk's salmon quilt.
Pale mirage mirroring the pier.
Stirred …
I've spied a magic sky.

Elizabeth Pappas

# Dull Light of Autumn

129

Dull light of Autumn. Muted in sepia leaf tones.
Mists seep in, as you weep a deep damp sigh.

Elizabeth Pappas

# Summer Song

Early morning flies b-z-z-z,
Squawking gulls tune up, awaiting a conductor,
Waves pound like the clash of dampened cymbals
and already the sun is striking with incisive rays.

      Wet crusty sand
      Beneath a hot body –
             cool.
      Hot sifted sand
      Beneath a glistening salty body
         real cool.

Lefki Kailis

# Autumn

Paper-nautilus leaves
s-lipping from the trees
zigzagging to and fro
I love to see them go.
They drift like
wafting feathers in a breeze.


Lefki Kailis

# The Variegated Acalypha

Look at it!
That asymmetric vibrant splash of colour,
its veins intent on knitting it together,
they tilt it tenderly towards the sun –
its God.

Lefki Kailis

# Winter Waterfalls

Spatter, swish, clear.

Spatter, swish, clear.

As the windscreen wipers dance to the rhythm of the blinding rain's beat, the car hurtles towards Mundaring Weir, delicately winding and weaving its way along the road of the same name, to the gathering masses.

September 1996

Spring's beginnings: but a winter's reward is manifesting in a whooshing waterfall of wonder, cascading in an endless torrent down that Mundaring Weir Wall, into the Helena Valley below.

Magical, masterful, memorable, as life's indispensable liquid journeys on its thirst-quenching trek through C.Y. O'Connor's masterpiece. This overflowing of Mundaring Weir is rare, an event for a lifetime memory.

We arrive. Our jalopy joggles for a niche in the tiny car park. The rain eases and our hearts dash with joy as our trio of hubby John, our son, Phillip and I, are swept up in the moment of this phenomenon seldom seen in Perth. We are at one with the amassed throng, delighting and relishing in this awe-inspiring spectacle.

Mundaring Weir is awash. Awash with pure, wet, unadulterated water. It has rained, then rained again, then rained some more. This usually stagnant and concrete monolith transformed into a cataract of nature's natural beauty.

These rapids, created by a winter's ending to a parched summer.
Beautiful.
Solid concrete transformed into a flushing field of lusciousness.
Beautiful.
Heaven's rainbow intermingling with this falling deluge.
Beautiful.


Lacey Healey

# Autumn

You rescue us from summer's searing heat
No longer do we need to beg for relief.
Like a warm and friendly guest you arrive
We feel your warm kiss upon our cheeks.

We witness you disrobing from your summer green
Revealing splendid garments of gold, orange and scarlet
Later to scatter them from your boughs
Becoming a colourful blanket upon earth.

Autumn showers bring welcome relief
The flora all sing in chorus
The sweet smell of the once parched earth fills our lungs
Giving rise to our sense of connection.

Fresh green pastures
Animals gently grazing
The brook is again alive and babbling
Autumn crocus herald your arrival.

The beauty of Autumn brings much to admire
En masse in our vineyards and orchards
Displayed there in their Autumn finery
Until dormancy comes as Winter approaches.

Dorothy Littmann

# Soft Shaft of Sunlight

Soft shaft of sunlight.
So silent in your reserved approach.
Consummating with brief fingers, my winter.


Elizabeth Pappas

# Birds

Birds on the sandbank
Musing by the tide.
Hoisted suddenly by the wind …
Arrowing into clouds, then they are gone …

Elizabeth Pappas

# Weeping Willow

Weeping willow you look so sad
Weeping willow are you so bad?
Your roots spread and problems cause
Should I tear you down, or stop and pause?
Invading gardens in search of water
Sometimes causing a real disaster
Invading pipes for the water you thirst
You are a naughty tree but not the worst
Your wood is weak and it may drop
When storms of winter swirl you like a mop
Graceful branches swaying in the breeze
Who visits you, well not the bees
You gently droop your leaves so small
But when Autumn comes those leaves don't fall
The winds of winter blow cold air
You weather them all without a care
And when again Spring comes round
You are still there in the warming ground
Weeping willow so lovely to see
Keep on weeping just for me.

Elaine Palassis

# PONDERINGS

# Kindnesses

## Floral Tribute

On driving to Albany from Muchea for my brother's funeral, I had allowed plenty of time for unexpected contingencies. There were none, and thus I stopped at the servo restrooms to apply fresh make-up for the harrowing day ahead. My stuff was laid out at the sink mirror and inconvenienced another young lady user. I apologised and explained I was putting on my 'brave face' for the sad day ahead. She smiled empathetically and left.

Moments later, she returned with a posy of bright flowers being sold in the fast-food section, gave them to me and said they were for myself and brother at the funeral.

The unexpected kindness still evokes tears.

## Teenagers

Envisage an IGA in Midvale on a thirty-eight-plus degree day, with several young teenage boys quietly skateboarding in the cool of shop aisles. They were doing no harm; it was not busy, and staff did not seem to object. I smiled at them and commented that it was a nifty way to do the shopping, please don't run over any grannies and that I should really try it sometime.

One mischievously asked me if I would like to try now and I thought why not, as good a time as any, before I really *am* too old.

Offer accepted. With much laughter, thoughtfulness, care,

enthusiasm, and moral and physical support, I was joyfully escorted down the dairy aisle by these cheeky, fun lads. They showed me where to place my feet and body for my very first skateboard effort.

It was one of those unique memories, moments of no expectations, connection and joy, without frills or premeditation. My eyes again mist as I write of this unexpected fun and kindness.

## Russian Invasion

I fell heavily at the Belmont Recycling Depot, sending a light box of aluminium cans flying. A nearby good-looking gentleman, forty-ish, with a strong Russian-type accent, hurried over to help me up; asked after my welfare and while I requested a moment to get my head and legs etc. together, he collected and re-boxed all the widely scattered cans from the carpark. He then gently and concernedly assisted me to the vertical. All ended well enough as I was only shaken, not really hurt. Now that was a man I was '*Russian*' to fall for.

## IGA Again

I sat on the bench outside the IGA, put my largish floppy bag at my feet and made a necessary complex phone call. I then rose to complete my shopping tasks. On entering the shop doors, a voice hailed me and as I turned, a man asked if this wallet was mine. This eighteen-ish Middle Eastern guy in the illustrious suburb of Belmont had seen the wallet slip out of my grounded bag, picked it up, and had pursued me in order to return it. Then he was gone. I was gobsmacked in gratitude. Restores one's faith in the world, don't it?

Hilary Williams

# **Con Dreams**

143

Con dreams of Delphi.
Evaluating his new blue and white tiled Como residence.
Kookaburras sit laughing on a marble sculpture of Athena.
Riven, I peer in passing at Parthenon pillars.
My shallow reserve thinks, it's never going to be an Onassis oasis.


Elizabeth Pappas

# I Dive Deep

I dive deep into myself.
Wrap my proud ego in compassion, for it might yet yield …
perhaps awaken.
I chant in rhythm with yellow-robed monks.
Perchance to glimpse Nirvana …

Elizabeth Pappas

# Time Ekes Out

145

While encompassing all,
time ekes out its moments.
But lodges nowhere … ever.


Elizabeth Pappas

# La Musica

Musica, you have inspired me so much
From early touch, my life was devoted to you
My ears fascinated by the sound of ivory keys
Even the hard work of practice didn't put me off
You have accompanied me all my life
Given me strength in hard times
The music of Bach transports me to higher spheres
Certain phrases by Mahler touch my soul
My inner ear has developed over the years
Even when I hear a sound or a little phrase
I can identify the composer and his work
Without you, Musica, my life would be empty
Beethoven said:
'Music is the mediator between the spiritual and the sensual life.'
And this is true to my life
Music is magic.

Ingrid Berchem

# Which Way the Wind Blows

I look up to the sky
I wet my finger and hold it up to the wind
Which way is it blowing today?
Do I venture out?

Will it be a smooth sunny day
Or a day of more rugged terrain
How will I know
Unless I put my foot outside the door

I don't need the daily weather report
My aching hips knees and hands
Tell me the real story
I need to listen, take heed of what they say

Some days the movements are easy
The sun is out, there is warmth in the air
There is a spring in the step
The mood is bright light and full of sunshine

But there are other days
When damp and cold descend from darkening skies
The body stiffens, slow to move
There is a cold contracting tightness

There can be abrupt changes day to day
Maybe four seasons in one day, perhaps more
The mood shifts from lightness to darkness
And back again, seeking out the light

Life and people can be like the weather, they intersect
Moodiness, grey skies, a feeling of darkness
Then the sun breaks through the clouds
And suddenly there is a glowing warmth, the mood has shifted

Predicting the changing patterns of weather and people
Can be like a pendulum swinging from side to side
The energy taking it wherever it needs to go
Maybe in circles, perhaps back and forth

Learn from nature that we cannot control everything
Be open to whatever winds of change are being presented
Learn to adapt quickly and with courage
Change is everywhere, nothing stands still, movement constant

The Earth is our Mother, our Guide, our abundant provider
Take care of her, she embraces us with her jewels
Wrap your arms around her with love and care
Our fate and destiny are in her hands.

Sam Ryan

# Predictable ... or not

I am PREDICTABLE
*Yet not predictable*
I am CONSERVATIVE
*Yet radical*
I am SOCIAL
*Yet solitary*
I am LOGICAL
*Yet contradictory*
I am OUTGOING
*Yet introverted*
I am OPEN
*Yet closed*
I am INVOLVED
*Yet detached*
I am HAPPY
*Yet sad*
I am AGREEABLE
*Yet peppery*
I am APPROACHABLE
*Yet elusive*
I am SEEN
*Yet not seen*
I am ALONE
*Yet not lonely*

I am one coin
*Yet I am head and tail*
I am only one
*Yet I am a mixture of many*

Predictability
Creates comfort for others
But behind the mask
Lies another not so predictable

Breaking out in small ways
So as to not disturb
Hampered by conditioning
Routines and social mores

Is all this the stuff of nightmares
Or simply the reality of life?

Sam Ryan

# Candle

The candle burns,
lithe flame flickering.
Pulling back, now incandescent
reaching upward, upward
with magnetic allure,
there my spirit goes.

Lefki Kailis

# Night

One by one they peel away
each to their own domain,
quiet beauty of night descends,
all to myself again.

Stealthily her power imbues me,
jettisons dry tired eyes,
slowly, slowly time eludes me,
my soul is free to fly.

Lefki Kailis

# Don't say Never

153

'Never, Never, Never, Never, Never …'
E–c–h–o–e–s and R–e–v–e–r–b–e–r–a–t–e–s.
Not spreading, but repressing,
Not giving, but shrinking –
Not doing, not saying
Not seeing …
Dying.

Lefki Kailis

# The Broca Area

The avid reader that I am stumbles on sentimental stories that move one, but discoveries are also made. This is how I stumbled onto the 'Broca' area; it is the frontal area of the brain responsible for language and mouth's motor movements.

Over the years my Broca has had a busy time. I was born in Lausanne on Lake Geneva. My first language was French, however, WW2 disrupted family life and we four kids had to be farmed out to grandparents, uncles, and aunts. Mother Lydia and I ended up with Uncle Hans and Aunt Frieda and three cousins, all girls! I reckon that I was well looked after with them, but had to switch to 'Switzer Deutsch,' the Swiss German dialect. This proved to be handy as it prepared me for primary school to speak 'Hoch Deutsch,' the proper German. Some of this Hoch Deutsch still surfaces every so often.

Then the whole family ached to return to Lake Geneva and to speaking French. We moved and ended up in Vevey on the lake. This language switching stirred up the desire to learn English. During my last year in High School, I gave up my free Wednesday afternoons to attend English classes. My four-years older sister, Marlyse, showed me the way by spending a year in England as an au pair learning the language. I prepared my escape by finishing my apprenticeship then mapping out my next move.

Everything happened as we would have wished! My wife Denise and I arrived in Houston, Texas in 1964 where I learned to speak their version of English. Luckily the Southern drawl hasn't stayed on my tongue or Broca. One of my clients there, came from an old Louisiana family which spoke French from two centuries ago! Oh, I loved hearing it. Later, several years in New Zealand polished off any vestiges of my American accent. Then up in the Cape York Peninsula I was to hear in the Aboriginal communities, other adaptations of the English language. Sometimes, I use one of their expressions to mark a treasured book:

'Him belongem to François.'

And then there is the language of the Australian outback with which Hilary, a member of Chapters, keeps us up to date.

The other example of language adaptation I love is 'Seselwa,' the Seychelles version of French with the inclusion of some African expressions and eliminations, the French complications of gender, articles and so on. And of course, inclusion of English making their language a language that suits their Broca. My Broca, however, didn't take to the Chinese language. After spending a year and a half in Wuhan and Nanyang, I can say hello: 'nichau' and thank you: 'siese ni,' but not much else remains! The fault is my increasing 'poetic dispersion,' memory loss in other words. Fortunately, my present wife Aline and I overcame this by spiking our conversation with words from three languages. This has been written in messy longhand cribbled with mistakes, thanks to the computer's spellcheck it is now readable. If all this makes some sense, I say: 'Thank you, Broca'.

François Jan

# My Perfumed Life ... ...

In my kitchen I am cooking
Tomatoes and garlic are simmering
Cookies baking in the oven
Vanilla cookies by the dozen
So hazelnuts I need to roast
For those cookies I love most
Evening in Paris a perfume preferred by my mother
Though not the gift of Chanel No 5 from my brother
I remember my mother with a sense of doom
The day she went to the emergency room
Remembered perfumes in my life
The day I became my husband's wife
That day he sent me a gift of scent
For me to wear to our special event
Other smells and perfumes too
Some for people and some for the loo
The heavenly smell of my newborn's head
The joy of seeing them sleeping in their bed
We live by the seashore so lots of wind
Sun and breezes will dry the bed linen
So a fresh lemon I need to slice
To squeeze over my fish pies
I love the feel of the wind in my face
When the wind and rain make me race
Out to the seashore to walk and ponder
Is there a better smell I wonder.

The smell of fresh salty air
I enjoy all without care
But it's time to get back to home
All will be there tomorrow for me to roam.
My cookies are cooling, the fish pie too
The hazelnut ones are almost due
The lemon is now on the pie
It's all so pleasing to my eye
The family soon will be in this room
With all their scents to lighten the gloom.
The door has opened and all rush in
I love the mess and all that din.
Makes me know I am alive
Knowing my love will help them thrive.

Elaine Palassis

# Connections

What brings me and makes me alive?

Let's take the Harp as a Symbol for these connections.

The Harp has 47 strings. When plucked they produce a beautiful sound, and each string vibrates.

When I meet a person and start a conversation, I'm lucky if there are two strings plucked so we have a view to things in common.

But when I sit in the lounge of the Concert Hall and start a conversation with a stranger and find that we are touching together several strings 'Wow!' We have many things in common.

It is not very often, that you find someone who is able to pluck many strings, but good friends together can bring out in me, or you, what is dormant and makes me alive.

Ingrid Berchem.

# The Dance of the Human Mind

It is like little insects trying
To crawl in all the corners
Of the brain in search of the
Inner self.

They dance, dance and dance
Must use their snow-white tutus
To cover up the
Outer World
To find the
Inner self
The door to God.

Ingrid Berchem

# Shades of Night

I choose to water them at midnight
My dolphin vines, ruby belle,
My eucalypt
I write a letter to my daughter –
still in the stars,
Whisper dreams into a blue cup of water.
And she is there,
the Moon –
behind the glass door
Veiled in white plume
In the navy shade –
Still,
Watching over invisible currents fade.

Hush,
Listen –
A woman grieves her lost dreams –
Etches them in stone.
Versed in defeat,
That is no fault of her own.

A girl imagines life and love
Maps out the veins to her heart
In a fit of youth
She trembles – ready to start.

I hear
hushed blue streams
Tears and dreams possess the swollen air
And she is there,
The moon
Behind the glass door
evolving in ghosts of blue
Still,
Heavenly, a drop of dew
Shrouded in white veil
My dolphin vine, red ruby belle
My forest green eucalypt
And I, accustomed to the blue
Of midnight.


Kritika Lama

# Hallelujah

Rejoice fellow creatives
let your energy flow

your light shine
and your spirit soar
to embrace Divinity.

Alas we are one
in this sacred space
united by the written word

HA – LLE – LU –JAH.

Mimma Tornatora

# Dazzling

A dazzle here a dazzle there
Dazzles come from everywhere
Who will dazzle who will not?
Some dazzles win, some will rot
So what is a dazzle one might say?
A dazzle is something to brighten your day
Does a dazzle make you smile you ask?
Or does your face remain a mask
Does the dazzle make you really mad?
Well it can you know if you are sad
And so miserable you want to wallow
You are so sad you cannot swallow
Life is all about ups and downs
And sometimes you want to kill those clowns
Who want to dazzle and smile and play
To put off your woes for another day
So it's time to dazzle and be a bit mad
Its time to dazzle and not be sad
For tomorrow is another day
Well that's what those who dazzle say
Now it's time to dazzle and let it be
It's time to dazzle for all to see
So let your dazzle beat that karma
For which there is very little armour
You can dazzle anywhere
So dazzle dazzle everywhere.

Elaine Palassis

# Attitude, Gratitude

Attitude, gratitude: to which my devious mind added 'platitude.' This platitude immediately provoked a song, of course.

'Please forgive this platitude, but I like your attitude.'

My immense gratitude to singers, composers, and lyricists for all these short stanzas that find their way into my brain. There isn't a day or night without a song. In my late teens, a new sound, the advent of 'Modern Jazz' took place. The sound of the Modern Jazz Quartet, Jerry Mulligan, Miles Davis, and others captured me. These, mainly quartets, all had strong bass lines that moved me. I was ever so grateful to be able to scratch enough money together to buy a big contra bass. I took to it like I don't know what. Martial, my excellent drummer mate, found a just as excellent tenor sax player. So, we had a trio and found a place to rehearse without upsetting the whole neighbourhood. In a few months we gelled sufficiently to play a few gigs at a Youth Centre. Oh, I enjoyed the attitude of the girls in the audience making my girlfriend rather jealous.

It is indeed said that all good things come to an end. The desire to travel overtook me, and I had to separate myself from my bass, too huge to fly about with me. I left it with immense gratitude for the two to three years we had strung strings together. However, the song: 'Rhythm of Life' gratefully still lightens my attitude to life.

If you are still reading these platitudes, I'm appreciative of your benign attitude with gratitude.

François Jan

# Special Bonding

Acquaintances they come and go
But forever friends are best to know
They are always there when things are down
To soothe away your fears and frowns
Likewise you too do the same
There's perfect trust and never blame.

Pure rapture enfolds over the years
Capturing shared joys and on occasion some tears
Relating together whatever outcomes
You'd lay down your life for them
That's how strong love becomes.

Lynette-Kay Lewis

# Sands of Time

How vastly desert waste in barrenness sorely be
Where patterns do portray the pace
Of windswept sandy spree
The grains of sand in ripples form
Like tossed upon the strand
Expressions of inspired design
Etched like by artist's hand.

How surely shifting endlessly
The patterns form and go
Like thoughts upon our tiny minds
In endless to and fro.
The ripples of the mind thoughts
Most holy … some quagmire
Those buried deep
From whence they form.

We have yet to understand
We'll keep only those that inspire
Instead of dire quicksand.
How likened to the desert land
We fashion our full thought
From endless sea of shapelessness
Is wrought what ere we ought.

Let us leave impressions
Of footsteps tried and true
Encompassing those future-born
That they will know … so true
Inspiring them to understand
From of essence our lives brought
If we've yet come to only nought
But as echoes left so grand
We've left our marks as encouragement
'pon shifting history's sand.


Lynette-Kay Lewis.

# In a Flash of Clarity

Oh, how I wish my brain was clear
It's not like I've been drinking beer.
My mind is in a moment of freeze
Have I dementia or Alzheimer's disease?

In a flash I need absolute clarity
To speak clearly to this important charity.
The sentences have left my head
And my words are forgotten and mumbled instead.

Was speaking too fast causing my confusion?
Or am I experiencing some delusion?
The members listening were smirking and nodding
I guess they're wondering whether to do some prodding.

Then all of a sudden, a light flashed in my brain
And back on track I launched again.
Now explicit and easy to understand
As the main presenter, I was in demand.

The audience digested this charity chat
Some even stood up and raised their hat.
There is no doubt left in my mind
How such a flash of clarity was instantly kind.

Kerry Smith

# Seventeen Champagne Glasses ...

Earlier this week I opened a kitchen cupboard that I do not use very often, and found seventeen champagne glasses. This has caused some quite serious pondering over the week: what sort of woman (other than Paris Hilton perhaps) needs seventeen champagne glasses? There is no mixture of red wine or white wine glasses (and I can barely remember the difference anyway) but whatever possessed me to acquire so many? It is not as if I have had big celebrations at any time, such as a 21st or a major wedding anniversary. There they sit, lightly dust-covered, in several matching groups, just keeping their own counsel. Why do I need seventeen of them?

I am in the process of going through every cupboard, shelf and corner in my home, rooting out anything I have not used in a year, and imposing onto friends, gifts that consist solely of books, scarves, handbags and shoes ... ah yes! The *shoes*.

If I were the sort of woman who becomes deeply thoughtful over seventeen champagne glasses, you would likely think that I could become almost hysterical over nearly fifty pairs of shoes, wouldn't you? And yes, I did say *fifty* pairs. There they are, in boxes, shoe bags, shopping bags and some bare to the world, crammed into shelf after shelf of the wardrobe. There are the boots, some thigh high and others grim work-a-day in the salt mines kind. There are low-cut court shoes in glorious colours. And then the sandals, oh, the *sandals!* Pair after pair of sexy, skinny, glittery and witty sandals. Some are heeled sky high and others flat to the floor. There are lesser numbers of trainers, but there they are, one in slinky pink with a recognisable name tag.

After all, like most other people, I only have two legs – why do I need fifty pairs of shoes?

I can't get as far as this and not mention the books; painful as the introspection may be. When I left London to live permanently in Perth back in 2004, I brokenheartedly gave away hundreds of books that I would not be taking with me: some to libraries, some to friends and some, sadly, left on the verge in the hope that some kind soul may give them a home. This process was so painful that I promised myself that it would never happen again: from now on I would read only library books and newspapers. I truly believed that I had been adhering to this policy until this morning, when I *accidently* looked at the two big bookcases in my home (obviously not counting the small bedroom bookcases, of course), and found them stuffed to the limits. Somebody has obviously been into my home, quietly filling up empty, pure and vacant shelves. The range is breathtaking: everything from sickly love stories to vast tomes about … just about anything. Who could have done this to me? And what am I going to do about it? Obviously, another major cull is on the way. But *WAIT!* Am I sure that I have read them all? Better check again, I couldn't possibly get rid of an unread book, could I?

So, seventeen champagne glasses barely merit a mention when compared to three bookcases, do they? Still, maybe there is an answer: maybe I could use the glasses, drinking champagne to keep my spirits up while working my way through all those books.

Cheers!


Susan Ormrod

# Short Autobiographies

## John Baldock

I feature mainly as a visual artist, holding many art exhibitions worldwide. I have held lecturing positions in Fine Art, and have published a book on Creativity called *'God can be Downloaded.'*
I write poetry and articles for publication.
I work as a Psychotherapist in the Jungian Tradition.

## Ingrid Berchem

Music, travel, nature and people are the cornerstones of my life. I believe that *silence* is an important ingredient of all these loves of mine. And in poetry or prose I can go deeper into the meaning of words.
Chapters is an eyeopener to so many aspects of my life and I'm so happy to belong to this group.

## Moira Clancy

I was born in England in 1949, married in 1969, and emigrated to Australia, in 1972. Then had two children before returning to work in Child Protection and Juvenile Justice. I have a Batchelor of Arts in Justice Studies and after retiring was introduced to Chapters. Listening to the works of the talented writers who attend this group is most enjoyable and it has helped me to improve the quality and quantity of my own writing.

# Noeline Frost

I was married in Palmerston North NZ and my husband and I lived in Cambridge for fifteen years before moving to Perth. We returned to NZ when my husband became ill and later died. After an eight-year absence I have recently returned to live in Perth. While living in Australia I attended several courses at the university mainly to do with Parent Effectiveness Training. I also did an instructors' course on P.E.T. and Effectiveness Training for Women. As well as this a summer course on Transactional Analysis for Everyday Living, plus a seminar run by Mary Goulding on her book *Love is Almost Enough*, and several other types of seminars. I have three children, two girls and a boy, two of whom still live in Perth. I am interested in art, travelling and anything that broadens my horizons.


# Lacey Healey

Born in 1953 and raised in the leafy western suburbs of Perth, I can't remember a time when my imagination has not run wild. Stepping into my seventies, I reflect on my childhood, inventing scenes from TV shows and movies and play acting them in our backyard. I feel this has nurtured a love of writing for the screen. In 2017, I fortunately met Libby Pappas who proposed the idea of starting a casual writing group where writers could meet informally, share stories and offer moral support for an often solitary exercise. It was an immediate '*YES*' from me, Chapters was born, and from those humble beginnings, is now a huge success. It has been a wonderful outreach for me, both for writing and making some amazing lifelong friendships.

## François Jan

I have had a very interesting life, having lived in many different countries, meeting a vast collection of varied and interesting people, and sharing in a multitude of stories evolving from all of these experiences. At Chapters, I have relished the opportunity to record some of these, and have enjoyed telling them to my fellow writers.

## Lefki Kailis

It's travel, adventures, nature, a love of literature and language that inform my writing. Sometimes sitting on the terrace observing the interplay of wattlebirds and their cheeky little competitors the New Holland honeyeaters is enough to set me writing.

## Kritika Lama

Since as far back as I can remember, I've always loved books, literature, poetry and stories. My best memories from childhood were set in the library with my mother, an intermittent writer, whom I credit with ingraining in me the love of beautiful words. I love writing poetry because I can really play with words, run with the metaphors, and create a story for my inner life and musings.

I adore lengthening the feeling of a simple everyday emotion or situation and giving it a form that is lyrical.

# Lynette-Kay Lewis

Away from the solitude of hours of words written, to again enjoying Chapters, is a rewarding balance. Like-minds in rapport buzz with excitement. Being in such camaraderie, again to share, is very uplifting.

# Dorothy Littmann

I am now in my 84th year and have been writing for about 4 years. This gives me great pleasure and brings me in contact with other fun loving and talented folk. I live on a few little acres in the hills of Perth and much of my work entails capturing words to express the beauty of my surroundings. I feel this stage of my life has been refreshed by turning my thoughts and observations into a written piece.

# PJ Mistilis

I have always loved reading. I have also written two books, a screenplay and a textbook, which I self-published, and which was very successful, going into its third edition. Additionally, I made a children's game about health which was loved by all the health bodies in W.A. but which I found too hard to market. As the Sesquicentennial of Western Australia approached, I organised and produced a set of six commemorative porcelain plates depicting places of note in the state, to mark the occasion. One of these was bought by the WA government to present to Princess Anne when she visited in 1979.

I now, however, feel a pressing need to record at least some of the history of my family so that it will not be lost to succeeding generations.

# Robert Nelson

My life has been an adventure. I was fortunate to have been paid to see Western Australia via one of my careers, and to have passed through all but seven towns in Western Australia. I then ventured forth to see some of the rest of the world where many people never go. Just to live life to the fullest is such a joy to one's heart, and to live in the moment. Like watching a wall of water come over a waterfall which was only a trickle only moments before, and seeing a whale feed her baby. How lucky have I been?

# Susan Ormrod

I was a London born war baby; raised in various parts of Africa, including Cape Town with its mountains and seas; and Rhodesia and Zambia with none of those things, but with plenty of other interesting features. I then thrived working in several different countries before settling in peaceful Perth, where writing helps to make some sense of it all. I'm still working on that, and I'm cautiously beginning to believe that the travel bug is finally fully fed and satisfied.

# Elaine Palassis

As time passes, I find myself writing more and more poetry. I write very quickly and if the poem has not formed to my satisfaction within thirty minutes it will not be written. I find inspiration everywhere. It's a joy to be able to put the wanderings of my untidy mind on paper.

## Elizabeth Pappas

Here's me, having a ball as a writer … when I wonder why, it suddenly hits me. Chapters, of course! Six years and running … my tiny idea for a unique writers' group has blossomed into the magic it is today … a weekly gathering of tenacious, fun-loving writers. Lynette-Kay and Lacey, all those years ago, you stood by me. You know what, I reckon we 'done good!' I'm proud of all our group; your efforts, support and creativity make it what it is today. Absolutely Fabulous!

## Helen Pears

I have always been totally captivated by stories. I taught Literature for many years. It is my greatest joy to be able to share the love of stories with my little grandson.
A chance meeting in the supermarket looking for pimentos has led me to Chapters and this vibrant group of creative writers. It has given my creative writing purpose. I love it!

## Marie-Anne Pontré

Like my ancestors before me who settled in Mauritius, where I was born, I travelled far and wide with my husband, before calling Australia home in July 1978. My love of writing began in Primary School when I fell in love with a blue fountain pen, leading me eventually to become a High School teacher, teaching French and Home Economics in a Private School. After raising two lovely sons, I was blessed with four gorgeous grandchildren and grandmother duties. My love of languages and words propelled me into more personal writing until I discovered Chapters in early 2023 and realized that this was the place for me to be.

# Irene M Powell

If I was a weather report, I would be described as temperate with seasonal changes. There are marked changes in the air, spring is fresh and breezy. Summer can be sultry, but generally sunny. Autumn marks gathering mists and nut storing, while winter demands hibernation. Expect unexpected (and unexplained) seasons of chill and ice, which thaw following a few rays of sunshine. Fortunately, these are rare, but beware the storm clouds. Expect thunder, lightning, strong winds, and heavy downpours. Best to evacuate till it all blows over.

# Sam Ryan

I have a fascination with words that with my imagination I can turn into sentences, line after line, then into paragraphs and chapters. It is a magical process to see a story evolve or lines of poetry appear; to know that the thoughts and ideas that I have expressed on the page may resonate to give some joyful delight or perhaps a little insight to the reader of those words. I find that writing is a mysterious and pleasurable journey, and it gives a wonderful breadth of meaning to my daily life. I feel privileged to be able to express myself in this way.

# Kerry Smith

I have always loved to write, especially poetry. Being a passionate teacher and making a difference with children as creative writers, has always inspired me. Now, joining Chapters, it is my turn to experience the fun and creativity of many talented adult writers.

## Mimma Tornatora

I found Chapters purely by accident in 2023 and haven't looked back. I thoroughly enjoy the eclectic diversity of my newfound writing tribe, mixing with like-minded people and sharing quality work. I am a creative soul with a passion for poetry. I also write reflective narratives and social history. My motto is: *Whatever you do, keep it creative!*

## Pauline Weir

I am a numbers nerd, but amongst my finest achievements I include being born at all, being born in Perth in the naughty-forties when medicine began to mean something, choosing the best parents, marrying the right man which led to 56 years of married bliss and resulted in three children and five grandchildren, managing to successfully combine parenting with a career, whilst avoiding serious health issues, travelling far and wide when opportunities presented while still remaining on speaking terms with family members and friends. Oh! Yes! And finally getting around to sorting out my kitchen cutlery drawer.

## Hilary Williams

Life needs a smile, commonsense and adventure, wherever you live, whoever you are or whatever you do. Our world experiences are infinitely varied, but this does not preclude imagination, sensitivity, observation or passion. I hope my various contributions embrace this spectrum with some impact and brevity.

# Acknowledgements

We wish to acknowledge the valuable contribution of all those who have assisted us in this venture. There has been financial, professional and in-kind help to make this project possible. We would like to extend our thanks to Siena's Pizzeria-Ristorante-Caffe of Leederville for their generous and continued support of our ventures.

A big thank you to our tireless editors and for the professional finish of the compilation of our submissions.

We particularly wish to thank the friendly staff of Connect Victoria Park, our local community hub, for their help, and for providing us with a warm and inviting venue for our meeting each Friday.

We also wish to thank Helen Iles for her invaluable advice and publishing skills.

**Elizabeth Pappas**

Founder of Chapters Writers

Photograph: Mark Pappas